FACING THE CHALLENGE

RANDY ROMAIN

Copyright Randy Romain 2012

ALL RIGHTS RESERVED.

No part of this publication may be reproduced, stored in a retrieval system, or transmitted in any form or by any means, electronic, mechanical, photocopying, recording or otherwise without written permission of the publisher or author.

ISBN 978-1619271159

Dedication

To long-lost friends and acquaintances: to my young disabled peers stuck in institutions, to the support workers whose friendships enriched my life; to those who sought independence and made it possible for me to dream; and to my wife, Maura, for making my dreams come true.

Acknowledgments

In writing this book, I realized the impact the people I encountered had on me over the years. The people who built my self-esteem and those who tore it down.

First, I want to acknowledge the technical support I received from the rehab centers in Montréal and Ottawa, as well as the Louis Braille Society and the CNIB. They opened up a whole world to me and because of the technology they taught me, I was able to write this book.

I would also like to thank the many people who befriended me throughout the years. The people at rehab and long-term care who went above and beyond their duties; the occupational therapists who went outside their boxes to find ways to grow my independence; and my closest and dearest friends, Vicky Viale, Jocelyn Laniel, and Chantal Vaillancourt, whom I can always count on.

I am so grateful to those who helped me make this book a reality: my Aunt Elaine Denault and Cousin Gale Bartolo, Ruth Mohammed, Seaward Higdon, Dian Yu and Sigrid Macdonald.

I send special thanks to my nephew, Victor Athayde, for his technical support and to my wife, Maura, the most beautiful woman in my world!

Prologue

My purpose behind writing this is to encourage people who are faced with a problem (medical or otherwise) to face it, no matter how difficult it may be, and to give you some insight into what it's like to live with a progressive and debilitating disease. We never know what life has in store for us; certainly, I didn't. However, it's more gratifying to fight than to surrender to fears and to the unknown. I believe we have all been put on this earth to teach and to learn. It's my way to justify my existence. There is always hope.

September 2, 2010: Today is my birthday. I am presently fifty-two years old. I am married to an amazing woman, whose name is Maura. I was born in 1958, in Fort-Coulonge, a small lumber town in the Pontiac County region of the province of Quebec, Canada.

I am a person who is blind, quadriplegic, and requires the use of a ventilator to breathe. I have a progressive illness that, ever since its onset, has been slowly destroying my health and robbing my autonomy. I wrote my story to give people some awareness about what it's like to live with such a condition. If you are interested in knowing more about me, then please read my story. It's a journey that will make you think about what's important in life.

Chapter 1

From what I can recall, I had a normal and well-adjusted childhood. I was the second of three boys. My brothers and I got along well; even though things got a little rowdy at times, we looked out for each other.

Around the age of twelve, I began to have difficulties with my vision. I first noticed it during my summer vacation in 1970. I joined a baseball team and the coach made me play outfield; that's when I first knew that there was something wrong with my eyesight. During our first game of the season, near the third inning, the player at bat from the opposite team hit a fly ball in my direction. I didn't see it coming until it was halfway toward me. By then, it was too late. I couldn't run fast enough to catch the ball. I was ashamed because my parents were watching in the bleachers. I made a stupid move, permitting one of the players on base to run home, thereby giving a point to our opponents. I was discouraged because my father was there and I wanted to make him proud of me.

In the fall, I became a member of the football team but that didn't go too well. I was playing quarterback; however, I found it hard to keep up with the plays. It seemed like it took me twice as much effort to get anything done, so I gave up. I wasn't having any pleasure and I didn't feel I could help the team.

I returned to school in September and that's when I realized I had a serious problem with my vision. I found it hard to see what was written in my exercise books and on the blackboard. I had to sit in the front row so I could see what the teacher was writing. I was scared. I knew there was something wrong but I didn't want anyone to know. I was hoping it was a temporary thing and it would pass. Unfortunately, it wasn't so; things got worse. Along with my poor vision, I started to feel weakness in my legs and extremely tired. I had no energy at all. I was having severe anxiety attacks but I didn't know why. My heart was racing and I found it difficult to breathe. I felt awful! It got to the point where I was afraid to go to bed, yet I had to go earlier because I was exhausted. I would go to bed right after supper and fall asleep immediately, only to wake up sweaty, scared, and anxious.

During this difficult time, my report card arrived from school and my grades were bad. My parents were concerned about my poor performance and wanted to know why I was failing in most of my subjects; that's when I had no choice but to reveal my secret.

When I told them about my vision problems, my dad took out a bill from his wallet and said if I could identify it, he would give it to me. He was sitting approximately five feet from me at the kitchen table holding the money between his two hands. I tried my best to see what it was but I couldn't. That's when my parents realized there was something definitely wrong with me.

My mom took me to see an optometrist, who prescribed glasses for me. However, I wasn't happy because they made me look different from others. In spite of this, I tried to wear them for a while but they weren't improving my situation. My condition was deteriorating. My eyes were getting worse and my legs weaker. I began experiencing tingling in my fingers and toes. We went to see our family doctor. He told my mother to take me to Montréal to Sainte-Justine's Hospital; I needed to be seen right away by a specialist.

We boarded a plane to Montréal a couple of days after that and we took a taxi from the airport directly to Sainte-Justine's. It didn't take long for us to be seen; a nurse asked my mom a series of questions. It was a very confusing time. I was scared. I didn't know what was happening to my body. There were doctors, nurses, specialists, and technicians everywhere but no one was talking to me; no one asked me any questions. It was all about me but I felt like I was on the outside looking in.

A young doctor came and began to examine me. After checking me out from head to toe, he excused himself and said he would return shortly. He came back a few minutes later with two more doctors. They examined me thoroughly. After examining my eyes, the most senior of the three doctors asked my mother if I was on any kind of narcotics because my pupils were extremely dilated. My mother reassured him I wasn't on any drugs.

The doctors seemed baffled; they didn't know what was ailing me. They had a conversation with my mother and they agreed I should be admitted to the hospital so I could undergo a battery of tests to find out what was making me ill. I wasn't too happy about their decision but I had no other choice. If I wanted to get better, I had to stay and take my medicine.

I stayed at Sainte-Justine's for approximately three months. I underwent every type of exam imaginable. Some of them were tremendously uncomfortable and some were downright painful; strangely, my condition somehow improved while there. My legs and eyes got a little better than when I was admitted. Because of this, the hospital released me and sent me back home, without further diagnosis or treatment. I was really pleased to get out of there. I was never away from home for so long; I was glad to see my father and brothers because I hadn't seen them for months.

Upon my return home, I resumed my studies. I realized things were more difficult than before. I was having trouble reading and writing. I had a hard time when writing to keep a straight line and everything I tried to read was a blur. It took me a long time to focus on what was written on paper or on the blackboard. I couldn't keep up with everyone or everything.

My school was approximately a kilometer and a half away from our home, which meant I had to wake up earlier than everyone else to wash, eat, and get dressed so I could leave the house before my brothers, or I wouldn't make it on time. From the onset of my illness, everything I did required more effort but I never stopped trying to keep up. I didn't want people to know I was sick or to be treated differently. I just wanted to be a normal kid.

I always tried to conceal the fact I had low vision. I didn't reveal it to anyone except my closest friends. I felt embarrassed. I didn't want to be pitied.

I managed to get through that school year but it wasn't easy. My class work was a burden and I couldn't keep up. It made me depressed and anxious, and it was impossible for me to get everything done. If I had a book assignment, I only read bits and pieces to get an idea of what the story was about. If I had an exam and it was a multiple choice, I started to read the questions and when I ran out of time, I randomly picked a letter and hoped I chose the right one. Before I became ill, I enjoyed school. Learning for me was a pleasure; but after I got sick, it was a nightmare.

During that period, my parents announced, while having supper one evening that we would be moving soon to a small town in the Laurentians. It was completely unexpected. This meant more changes for me. Everything was happening at the same time and the move was one more thing I needed to come to terms with.

My father left a week before us to arrange everything. He had to find us a place to stay and go to school. I liked the town we were already living in. Everybody knew each other and was a friend. I really didn't want to start over.

Before leaving, we stopped to say our goodbyes to our neighbors and good friends. It wasn't easy. I had my heart in my throat and did my best not to cry, but we had to go. I felt a deep feeling of emptiness upon our departure. It was hard for me to accept.

Chapter 2

My dad came back to get us with a camping trailer. The plan was for us to live in the trailer until everything was organized and we could move into our new home. Where we were heading was far, so we stopped about halfway in a trailer park to spend the night. After eating, we retired for the night, and discovered, to our dismay, we were infested with small, black flies. They were all over us and ferocious. They bit and made us very itchy. It was simply unbearable. It was impossible for any of us to sleep. My brothers and I decided we would sleep in the car with the windows and doors shut tight, so the bugs couldn't come in. It wasn't the greatest but at least we could get some sleep without being eaten alive by those little black pests.

My parents didn't have it so easy. The flies were so small, they infiltrated the window screens. They had to close all the windows and cover themselves from head to toe not to get bitten.

We got up at sunrise and my mom prepared us a small breakfast before going back on our road trip. The weather was just beautiful. The sun was shining and there wasn't a cloud in the sky. We couldn't have picked a better day to travel. After a while, we stopped at a roadside restaurant to have lunch. It felt good to get out of the car. It was comforting to fill our tummies with good food and drinks. Before heading back on the road, we were obligated to go to the toilet. My dad told us it would be better for us if we went then, when we had the opportunity, because he did not intend to stop every five minutes for us to go later on.

After being fully replenished, we continued on our way. I was tired. I closed my eyes and fell asleep for a while, and when I woke up we were already past Montréal and heading into the Laurentians area. We travelled down a small, narrow road and the scenery was just beautiful. The leaves were bright red and golden orange, and majestic mountains overlooked the dark blue water. We passed through a series of little villages and they were all very quaint. The houses were mostly from the age of our pioneers. The streets were filled with flowers and various sorts of greenery. There were plenty of old trees everywhere and from what I could see, the environment was absolutely picturesque.

We got to a part of the road where there was a high mountain on our right and a raging river on our left. It was quite a sight. The scenery continued on that way for a good forty-five minutes. We passed by a beautiful waterfall that cascaded down a rock cliff, and soon after we arrived at our destination. It was a small village perched at the top of a steep hill and our house was situated on the other side at the bottom left.

Our new house was wonderful. It had a huge landscape with a small barn in the backyard, with a few cows, chickens, and horses. It was like a paradise to me.

Our next door neighbor was the father of the person who we were renting the house from. He owned the barn and a large corral where his horses could graze and run free. Next to his house, he built an artificial lake and stocked it with red trout. He also had a small creek flowing through his land. It was incredible.

Our house was spectacular! It had all the latest in kitchen appliances and it was more spacious then we had ever had. It was modern in comparison to the other homes. It was like it didn't belong there. The architecture was in contrast with the surrounding environment. I was delighted! We couldn't move in right away because we had to wait for the movers to arrive with our clothing, furniture, and household equipment. It took them longer than anticipated. We had to remain in our trailer for an extra two days. It wasn't the best of arrangements. We were looking forward to their arrival because we didn't have any toilet or running water inside the trailer, which made things difficult. We had to go into the house to use the bathroom and to drink water.

Once the movers arrived, it didn't take us long to settle in. Our new place was homey — cozy, with more room to play and explore. I loved the horses and the other animals in the barn.

It took me and my brothers a few days to get the courage to go up the hill, into the heart of the village, to see if we could meet kids our age. We went looking, trying to find something interesting to do, but there wasn't much. There was a small family diner, a garage with a fishing store, a church and a little clothing store. We decided to go into the diner to have a drink and fries. It looked like a fun place and the waitress who came over to serve us was beautiful. She was a young redhead about sixteen. She asked if we were the new people who moved into the house down the hill. We told her that we were and she gave us a big smile. She took our order and returned shortly after. I asked her name. She told me Melissa and asked ours. She was surprised when we introduced ourselves because we all had English names. Upon hearing our response, she asked if we spoke English. We told her that we did indeed, so she said, "But you don't have any accent when you speak French." We discovered no one in the area spoke or understood a word of English. Before leaving the diner, we asked Melissa if there was anything around for young people to do. She told us there wasn't much there for kids to do except farming and fishing but, upon reflection, she said there was a small pool room where most kids hung out, so we went to check it out.

The pool room and local hang out was a room with a small Boston table, a large snooker table, a few benches, and a little table with four chairs. It looked like the owner transformed his garage into a small pool hall. We discovered if we needed a drink or goodies, we simply had to knock on the door of the proprietor and he would come out from the kitchen of his home to sell us whatever we asked for. I thought it was a strange arrangement. He didn't have a large variety of merchandise, just a few kinds of chips, chocolate bars, drinks, and assorted candies. There was a young boy there sitting alone eating potato chips and sipping on a pop. He told us what we needed to do if we wanted to shoot pool. His name was Guy. He was curious and asked us many questions. We told him who we were, where we lived, and before we left for supper, I invited Guy to come and see us. And he said that he would definitely come. We made it back just in time to eat. My mom was curious and wanted to know where we went and what we did. I told her I met a pleasant young boy and we invited him over to visit.

The next day, my new buddy came over in the afternoon. I was glad. He showed me around the village and took me to what he called his secret hiding place. He constructed a small cabin in the backwoods behind our house, on our neighbor's property, near a small stream. The afternoon went by so fast, the next thing we knew, it was already time for us to go home. I had quite a busy day. After supper, I was so tired I didn't feel like doing anything but staying home and watching TV. Guy must have been just as exhausted because I didn't hear from him until the next day.

One day, Guy invited me over to his house for supper and to meet his parents. He lived in a very old house built at the turn of the century, halfway up the hill from our home. I felt shy about going but went anyway. When I got there, I had two major surprises. The first one was how old his parents were. His father was in his late sixties and his mom in her mid-fifties. The second and best surprise was his sister. She came out of a room next to the one we were in. She was the beautiful redhead from the diner with the great smile. I couldn't have been more pleased.

We sat at the kitchen table while the mother finished preparing the supper. Guy's father started questioning me about my family. I told him everything he wanted to know and he seemed satisfied. All the time we were talking, I couldn't help but look at Melissa. I was completely mesmerized by her beauty. It was the first time I felt that way about a girl — what a strange feeling. I tried hard for them not to notice my discomfort, but I was sure that they all did, especially Melissa. What a stunner!

When supper was ready, Melissa got up to help her mother serve the meal and I couldn't stop looking at her, so much so that Guy was getting angry at me. He was trying to get my attention but all my thoughts were on his sister. He had to kick me under the table to get my attention.

We had a good meal. After supper, we went to sit in the living room while the women cleared the kitchen and washed the dishes. I offered to help but they categorically refused. I tried to insist but it was useless. They didn't want my help. I was disappointed because I was hoping to have the chance to spend some time close to Melissa. I hoped that once she was done in the kitchen she would come and sit with us in the living room, but I wasn't so lucky. After she finished, she gave her mom and dad a kiss and told them she wouldn't come back too late. I was disappointed to see her disappear so fast.

After Melissa left, Guy and I decided to head down to the local hang out to shoot pool. When we arrived, three girls were sitting at the table sipping on a soda. They were pleasant, but one in particular attracted me the most. Guy seemed to know them very well, so he asked if any of them would like to shoot some pool. The one that interested me was the first to say yes. I asked her name and she told me Carole. I told her mine and we decided we would play together as partners against Guy and her friend. We had a good time. I really liked my partner. She was pretty and had a good sense of humor. The more we interacted, the more I liked her but unfortunately, the time was getting late and we needed to go. I didn't really want to leave; I wanted to spend more time with Carole. Before going, I asked if I could see her again the next day. She told me she wasn't sure, but she would try her best to come and see me at the pool hall.

I left the pool hall happy. I liked Carole and the best part was that I was convinced that she liked me. On our way back home, I kept asking Guy questions about Carole. He was getting annoyed and told me to shut up because I was getting on his nerves.

The following day I went over to the pool room after supper, hoping to see Carole. I waited for her most of the evening but she didn't show up. She had me thinking all sorts of thoughts: did she like me? I thought that she did. Maybe she just couldn't make it? I didn't really know the answers, but I wanted to see her again because all I was thinking about was her and it was driving me mad.

It had been several days since my first encounter with Carole. I was keeping busy with Guy, doing all kinds of things like fishing, bicycling, and working on his secret hiding place. I almost gave up on Carole; then, one day we went to the pool room and she was there. Boy, I was happy to see her, and from the expression on her face, she was also glad to see me, although I was trying very hard not to let her know how much I missed her. She was with a friend. They were both sitting at the table, chatting. Guy and I asked if we could sit with them and they agreed. We weren't there long when the girls asked if we wanted to go for a walk. We gladly accepted. Guy was interested in Carole's friend, so we were both pleased to go.

We walked a lot and took advantage of the occasion to talk and get to know each other. After a while, we decided to sit underneath a tree in the school yard. Carole sat close to me. I felt awkward and I didn't know what to do. It was the first time I ever had those kinds of feelings for a girl. I had never really kissed anyone. By that time it was dark, and the weather was hot and muggy. Carole looked especially beautiful to me that night under the light of the moon. We stayed there under that old brown oak tree for a couple of hours and it was really enjoyable. The more I spent time with Carole, the more I liked her, and the more my desire to kiss her increased. The hour was getting late and I had to go home, but I wanted to kiss Carole goodnight before we departed. I wasn't sure how to go about it. We walked back together. Guy also walked Carole's friend back; however, fortunately for me, she didn't live in the same direction as we did. It gave me the chance to be alone with Carole. When we approached her house, she stopped and told me this was far enough. She didn't want her parents to find out she was with a boy, but before we said goodnight, I finally got up the courage to ask if I could kiss her. She told me she thought I would never ask. I kissed her and it was fantastic! I wanted more. We stayed there kissing for a good ten minutes I didn't want to leave. The more we kissed, the less I wanted to go.

I left her feeling like I was on top of the world. What a feeling. It was great. I went back home very happy. I never imagined a girl could make me feel that way. I often wondered what all the fuss was about. Well, now I knew. I was in love or at least I thought I was.

I spent the summer with Carole, and we got to know each other well. She taught me a lot. She was a beautiful girl and I never wanted to leave her. I was content just being with her. Guy wasn't happy that I was spending more time with Carole than with him, and he let me know on several occasions. He was angry with me for a while but I didn't blame him. I would have been just as angry myself if he had done that to me.

Later on that summer, my family planned to go on a camping trip for a week. I thought I would ask my parents if Guy could come with us. It took some persuasion but eventually they agreed. It was the first time Guy ever left home and he enjoyed his time away. I was also having fun, but I really missed Carole and I couldn't wait to get home. When I finally arrived back home, we made up for lost time. We stayed with each other as often as we could and relished every moment.

Summer was over, school was starting, and we had to take a bus to get there. The school was approximately fifteen kilometers away from our home. The bus picked us up at the door and dropped us right at the school. It was the first time I had to take a bus to school and I enjoyed the experience. After the first few days, I began to feel sick, and again I didn't know what was happening. I was getting unbearable headaches, I was sweating profusely and I had a strange, bitter taste in my mouth. No matter what I ate, everything tasted the same. I couldn't eat any more because the taste was making me nauseous. I had no energy at all and I felt totally exhausted. I just wanted to go home — to bed. One afternoon, I was so sick I couldn't stand it. I went to the principal's office and he called my house. My dad came to pick me up shortly after. When I got home, I went straight to bed and I slept until the next day. The following morning, I woke up and tried to stand and walk to the washroom, but I simply couldn't. I no longer had any strength in my legs. I tried a few times but I couldn't do it. I eventually gave up. I lowered myself off the edge of the bed and dragged myself over to the washroom. Once there, I managed to hoist myself on the toilet. I made it there just on time. Once done, I tried again to stand, but I couldn't. I was worried, so I lowered myself onto the floor and dragged myself into the living room. I had no more strength. I waited a few minutes before hoisting myself on the sofa. After a while, I tried several times to get up and walk, but it was impossible. I began to panic and cry because I didn't know what was happening. Eventually, my mom heard me and got up to see what was going on. When she arrived, I told her I couldn't walk and to turn on the light because I couldn't see. She said, "It's already light."

Chapter 3

My mom helped me to get washed and dressed quickly. She told my father and brothers she was taking me right away to Montréal, to the children's hospital. She quickly gave my dad and siblings instructions on what to do while we were away. Approximately two hours later, we were at the children's hospital. We went directly to the emergency ward. We waited a while to be seen because the place was extremely crowded.

After waiting forever, a nurse asked us to follow her. She showed us into a room and instructed us to wait. It felt like déjà-vu to me. A doctor came in, and asked specific questions to my mom and began examining me. He started looking into my eyes with an instrument that shined a very bright light. After he was done, he began poking me everywhere with different little instruments, at the same time asking what I could feel. Once he finished, he told my mother that I would have to be admitted in order for them to discover what was going on with me. I wasn't very happy about having to stay inside the hospital, but again, I didn't have any say. If I wanted my condition to improve, I had to comply with their decision.

Well. There I was again, in Montréal, alone in a strange and unfamiliar environment, and away from my family. After a couple of weeks, my grandmother came to Montréal to stay with her oldest sister. She could visit me every day, so I wouldn't feel so alone. It was comforting for me to have my nanny close by. My mom couldn't come to see me as frequently as she would have liked to, simply because she had to stay home and take care of the house. She couldn't leave my father alone with my brothers for very long because he couldn't handle it. My mother came whenever possible but it wasn't enough for me. I missed my family.

My time at the hospital was lonely. Even though I had my nanny there, I missed my family and friends. The doctors had me undergo every diagnostic exam available to them at the time. There was one in particular I will never forget. It hurt tremendously and I had to have it for the doctors to see if I had any abnormalities in my brain that could be the cause of my illness. The side effects were just awful. I was in bed for a week after. I couldn't move my head at all and I felt totally sick.

During my time in bed, there was a girl who frequently came to visit. She was a patient I befriended during my stay. Her name was Beverly. She was seventeen and she was in the hospital for cancer treatment. She was extremely nice. She took me under her wing. She told me she was an only child and wished that she had a little brother; therefore, she adopted me. It suited me just fine because I always wanted to have a sister. She took care of me most of the time while I was bedridden. She came and read comic books, and helped me with whatever I needed. She was an angel sent from heaven. The first morning the nurse got me out of bed, I felt really uncomfortable. I couldn't walk. She got a wheelchair to bring me over to the washroom to give me a bath. I was dizzy. My head was aching and sweat was pouring down my face. I thought I would pass out. I didn't have any strength or energy, but luckily, when we got there she had already prepared everything beforehand, so all she had to do was get me into the bathtub. A male orderly came and took me into his arms and placed me in the water. It took a while and I was suffering a lot. The water was a little too warm and it made me feel even sicker. I couldn't wait for it to be over. Once we were done, the nurse got the same orderly that put me in the bathtub to get me out. Only, this time he carried me straight from the washroom into my bed. It was an experience I will never forget.

The next day I was better. My appetite returned and my headache disappeared. I felt stronger and I had a lot more energy. After breakfast, I thought I would try to take a walk over to see Beverly. Her room was just a few doors down the hallway from mine. When I got there, her room was empty. I got a sick feeling in my stomach because I somehow knew Beverly was gone. I didn't know what to think about it. I didn't believe she would leave without saying goodbye. I asked a nurse, who was passing by in the corridor, if she knew where Beverly went. She told me Beverly left the day before. She confirmed my fear. Her response made me feel empty and sad. My friend was gone, and I didn't get the chance to thank her for all the love and attention that she gave me. It has been nice to have her around as a friend but unfortunately, I was left with only my nanny, who came over in the afternoon when I didn't have any appointments.

The hospital had a small arts and crafts department that was run by volunteers. They came twice a week and anyone who was able could go and make their own creations. I liked to go there when I had the chance because it helped pass the time and allowed me to escape from my worries.

There was a little girl there who caught my attention. She was around five or six years old, and had practically no hair on her head. She was a nice, energetic young girl and everything about her seemed normal, but the lack of hair. I found out from her mother she suffered from an uncommon syndrome. Her parents brought her to the doctor because of her unexplainable hair loss and after doing some routine exams, they found she had a big ball of hair in her stomach. Upon further investigation, they discovered that while she slept at night, she would pull out her hair and eat it. So, to prevent her from doing this, they made her sleep with a bathing cap. She also had to undergo an operation to remove the ball of hair from her stomach.

There was a young intern at the hospital who took a liking to me. One day, he came over to get me and brought me to his office. I thought he would examine me or something of the sort, but it wasn't so; he took out a box and asked if I knew how to play chess. I told him I didn't and he kindly offered to teach me how, so from then on, whenever he had some spare time, he came and got me and we played a game of chess. It was a lot of fun. I enjoyed those moments because they made me feel special.

One afternoon, the porter came to get me and brought me over to a small, brightly lit room. I was greeted by a woman who explained that she needed to take a few pictures. It would help the doctors to discover what was wrong with me. After she was done with her brief explanation, she asked me to remove my pajamas. I was nervous and having difficulty unbuttoning my top. The woman noticed and helped me. She quickly unbuttoned and took off my top. At the same time, another woman appeared from a back room to speak to her. As they were talking, she continued undressing me. She removed my pants and slipped off my underwear. I was shocked and embarrassed. There I was, completely naked, a skinny, undeveloped, prepubescent, thirteen year old boy, who normally felt extremely uncomfortable at the thought of anyone seeing me in the nude.

I felt violated! I didn't know what to do. The two women stopped talking, looked at me, and told me to stand in front of a large screen close to the back wall. There I was, standing completely naked, waiting, while they adjusted their camera. I was totally humiliated. Finally, after a few minutes, which seemed to me like an eternity, they started to take pictures of me in various degrading positions; while they were taking photos, I caught them on a few occasions whispering to each other and giggling. I can remember it like it was yesterday. I was angry and troubled because they had me in a vulnerable and compromising situation. I felt they had a lack of empathy and respect toward me. The entire ordeal lasted approximately twenty minutes. It never seemed to end but finally it did. The same woman who undressed me came over and helped to put on my clothes. I returned to my room ashamed and distressed. I never thought I would be put in such a shameful situation. It was definitely an incident that scarred and traumatized me. What angered me the most is that they didn't realize what they put me through.

Shortly after, I was released from the hospital. We were told by the doctors I suffered from a rare form of juvenile multiple sclerosis, and there wasn't any prognosis or treatment. I returned home not knowing what my future held in store but I knew it wouldn't be easy. I promised myself I would be strong and I would never give up. I would do my best to be like everyone else. I didn't want to be treated any different!

When I got back home, I got a pleasant surprise. My parents gave me a dog and he was beautiful. He was a timid, black Labrador retriever. When I first called him, he came over with his chin down and his tail between his legs. The poor thing was shaking like a leaf. He seemed so fragile.

I was told he was attacked by a porcupine. He had quills imbedded into his face and different parts of his body. The previous owner hung him up in the barn from a chain to pull out the quills with a set of pliers. He still had the burn marks of the chain on his body. I could also see the different areas where he had the quills. I was told his name was Blacky. It didn't take me too long to gain his confidence despite the traumatizing ordeal he went through. I gave him a lot of love and attention, and he turned out to be a good companion. He was no trouble at all, except for the odd time when he came back home with parts of a dead animal that he fetched from a nearby neighbor's farm.

One day, I returned home from school only to find the front yard draped with chicken feathers. There were feathers everywhere. I thought it to be natural — after all, he was only following his instinct — however, I believed it would be better if I got everything cleaned up before my parents could see it or else he would certainly be in trouble.

My biggest fear at school was when the teacher asked me to read something out loud in class. I would panic and everything went out of focus and I couldn't read. So, when the teacher asked us to write an essay and to read it out loud, I memorized what I wrote. I stood in front of everyone and pretended I was reading but, in reality, I was blurting it out by memory. I was careful not to make my reading look too easy, so I wouldn't draw suspicion. Surprisingly, I managed to pull through and get away with it.

I began having more problems. My legs and ankles were getting weaker, increasing my difficulty to walk. I got tired much easier and I had to be careful while walking not to twist my ankles. Walking for me was a calculated thing to do; I had to pay attention to every step I took. If I didn't, I would surely end up falling. I was also starting to have difficulty with my bladder. Sometimes, when I felt the urge to void, I had to go immediately but on other occasions, I could keep it in as long as I had to. No problem. Therefore, I got special permission from the school principal to let me leave the classroom whenever I needed to go.

My life changed. I was no longer the happy-go-lucky kid I used to be. I was often scared, anxious, and stressed but I tried hard not to let it show. I was a joker. Whenever I had a problem I laughed it off, but deep down inside, I wished I was normal. I didn't like to be different and I didn't want any special treatment.

I didn't know what would become of me: how my illness would progress, or how long I would live. I decided I wasn't going to spend my life worrying about the future and what might happen to me. I was going to take it as it comes. Every loss for me at that point became a challenge. I was determined to do my best to adapt by finding ways to compensate.

During the winter, there wasn't much to do but snowmobile and hanging out at the local pool hall. We went sometimes to play cards at our arts and crafts teacher's house. She was an eccentric lady. She let us do whatever we wanted. She liked to have a drink and smoke cigars. It was strange for me to have such an instructor. Out of school, she was teaching us things that weren't too "Catholic." She had a little shack behind her house, and inside it had a small wood stove, two bunk beds, a table and four chairs. It was pretty cozy. Our teacher gave us the run of the place. Whenever we wanted to go, we simply had to knock on her door and she gave us the key. We often went there to make out with the girls. I learned a lot about sex and girls inside that little shack.

One day I was snowmobiling with my little brother, Bruce, and a friend. Bruce was driving, our friend was sitting in the middle, and I was behind. The weather was stormy. It was windy and the snow was blowing in every direction. The visibility was poor. We were going up a steep hill behind the local outdoor skating rink. When we got to the top, we were struck by a snowmobile coming on our left. He was going fast and hit us hard. Upon impact, he hit my little buddy's leg and my own. The pain was excruciating! We were knocked off the vehicle into the snow and the person who hit us left the scene immediately. My little brother ran to get help. It took a while for help to arrive and for them to figure out what to do. They finally decided it was best to transfer us onto a sled and bring us in the little cabin beside the rink that was used as a change area. We were both in shock and shaking. We needed to get to a warm area and fast!

They carried my friend down first, and after what seemed to me like an eternity, they finally came for me. When they picked me up to put me on the sled, one of the people who lifted me clearly didn't know what he was doing. He grabbed me right where my leg was fractured. I let out a scream; it startled him and he let my leg drop on the side of the sled. I thought at that moment I would pass out. I felt sick to my stomach; I tried my best not to cry. It was sheer pride; I wanted to act tough in front of my peers. My little buddy was sobbing and moaning with agony. I felt sorry for him. Once we were in the change room, they put us down near the wood stove to keep us warm while we waited for the ambulance to arrive.

During that time, Bruce called home to tell my parents what happened. My mom and big brother, Chuck, hurried over to see me. I asked my brother why my dad wasn't with them. He told me Dad was sitting comfortably in front of the television, in his pajamas, watching the hockey game; I can remember feeling heartbroken at that moment by his response. I felt he didn't care enough for me to come to see how I was doing. It's something I will never forget. I loved my dad, but unfortunately, it was obvious he didn't love me enough to come to my side.

It took the ambulance over one hour to come. When the paramedics arrived, they stabilized my leg with an inflatable splint before moving me on to the stretcher. They did the same for my buddy. The closest hospital was approximately seventy kilometers away. The ride down was long and painful. The roads were bumpy and every time we hit a bump, it made my leg bounce, causing unbearable pain. We discovered, along the way, that the inflatable splint had a leak and it was completely deflated. I couldn't wait to get to the hospital.

Once we got there, I was brought to the emergency ward. I was seen by the triage nurse who sent me right away to the x-ray room. They transferred me from the stretcher onto the x-ray table. I had to endure, once again, the torture of them moving my leg. Once on the table, they slightly lifted my leg to get the x-ray chart under it and it was unbearable. After they were done, they transferred me back onto the stretcher and pushed me to the waiting room. The doctor arrived soon after. He told us I had a compound fracture of the tibia, and I had to stay overnight so they could repair my leg. They put a temporary cast to stabilize it until they could do the operation. I was placed on a ward in a private room. My mom left after verifying I was comfortable for the night.

The nurses who took care of me were attentive. They brought me a jug of cold water and a urinal. They gave me some medication to ease the pain and help me sleep. I woke up during the night with a strong urge to void. I quickly tried to grab the urinal but I couldn't make it on time. I began to void and I couldn't stop. I totally wet myself and the bed. I was ashamed and I didn't want the nurses to know, so I took the jug of cold water and spilt it on myself and the bed to hide the fact I was incontinent. After doing so, I rung my call bell to get help. A nurse came to see me right away. When she arrived, I told her that I accidentally spilled my water all over myself and the bed. She smiled and said, "No problem. Let me get some help and I will be right back."

She returned with another nurse, and had me and the bed changed in no time. It felt good to be warm and dry again.

The next morning I wasn't allowed to eat or drink because the doctors scheduled me to have the operation to repair my leg sometime during the afternoon. They finally came to get me around three. I was nervous but happy to go. I was starving and I couldn't wait to get it over with so I could eat. The operation went well; however, I was in pain. I don't know what they did but it hurt like hell! I was able to have a liquid diet later that evening. It wasn't much but it was better than nothing.

I went home the following day. My mom came to get me. I had a cast on my leg all the way up to my groin. I had to sit sideways on the backseat of the car, with my leg up on the seat, because it was swollen and painful. I found out upon my return that the person who struck us was Carole's older brother. I didn't hold it against him because, after all, it was an accident. He simply got scared, panicked, and left the scene. We were informed later the reason he ran was because he didn't have his license plates on his vehicle. Carole began to ignore me after that. I felt sad and disappointed. I didn't understand why, all of a sudden, she chose to distance herself from me.

Once I returned home, I resumed my schooling but it wasn't easy. I was having trouble with my eyesight, bladder, walking, and coordination. Taking the bus on crutches was hard. The laneway from the house to the road was on a steep slope, and getting from the house to the bus and off the bus was problematic most of the time. It was often draped with ice and snow. I frequently fell; even though I often got help from one of my brothers, we occasionally both ended up falling.

I dreaded going to school for all those reasons. It was a constant battle to do anything. I tried my hardest to keep up with everything, no matter what. What gave me comfort during those troubled times was Blacky. He was always there when I needed him and loved me unconditionally. He was truly my best friend. I didn't have to prove anything to him and he was there for me when I was down.

One month after my accident, I returned to the hospital to check if my leg was healing well. By the x-ray, the doctor told my mom and me it was healing fine, but I wasn't ready to have my cast removed. I wasn't too happy about that. I was hoping I could get it taken off, although I got some relief when they removed the full leg cast and put another one just below my knee, with a rubber heel, which enabled me to walk on it. It meant I no longer had to use those darn crutches! I was instructed to wait two days before walking on it. It had to be completely dry or else it would become too loose and it wouldn't properly protect my fractured bone.

The walking cast made it much easier to get around but it was messy. I had to be careful not to get it wet. It wasn't easy because we were already in mid-April and the weather was crazy. The ground surface wasn't good during that time. Even though I tried hard not to get my cast wet, it was virtually impossible. After a couple of weeks, my cast became soft and soggy, so I was forced to use my crutches again because it was falling apart. Luckily, I had an appointment to get my leg checked out in less than two weeks.

It wasn't a moment too soon. They took another x-ray of my leg and it wasn't quite healed. I had to go back home with another walking cast for at least an additional month. I was disappointed.

The new cast gave me problems. They put it up a little too high. Whenever I bent my knee, the cast cut into the back of my knee. It was most problematic during the night, while I was in bed. I would wake up in pain because the cast was digging in, causing my leg to contract and making the cast cut in deeper. My skin became raw. It went on like that for a week until I got fed up. I took a steel saw blade and cut my cast down a good four inches. That was enough to correct the problem.

Spring settled in and the weather was beautiful. I finally got my cast removed. What a relief. However, my left lower muscles, where I had the cast, shrunk. I tried very hard to exercise to increase them but the exercise had no effect whatsoever. Unfortunately, it was the same for the rest of my body. No matter how hard I worked out, it didn't change a thing. On the contrary, the more effort I put out, the weaker I got. It was discouraging. I tried my best not to let it get to me. I knew if I let my problems worry me, it would only make matters worse.

Despite my numerous struggles, I enjoyed life and the people that surrounded me; it was the reason why I never let go. I must say that I am thankful to my family for treating me like everyone else ever since the onset of my illness; by doing so, they encouraged me to go on. I truly believe if they had given me special treatment, I wouldn't have the resilience and strong mental capacity which I gained throughout the years.

One day during supper, my parents had another announcement. They informed us we were moving again soon but they weren't sure exactly when. They could only assure us that it wasn't before the school year ended. I didn't anticipate another move. We were going back to live in Buckingham, Québec, where we had previously lived seven years before. I was fourteen years old at the time, and to my brothers and me, it was almost like moving to a new city. We didn't have too much recollection about the people or the area. I decided I would try my best not to think about it until the time came.

One afternoon, I was bored sitting at home with nothing to do. I thought I could help around the house by cutting the grass, which needed a good trim. Things were going along just fine until I came to the side of the house where there was a steep slope. I was pulling the lawnmower up the hill when my left foot slipped under the mower. It was the same foot that was previously in a cast. My mom removed my running shoe and blood gushed everywhere. She feared the worst, but only the tip of my shoe was cut off and three of my toes were slashed. My big toe got the brunt of it and it gave me a burning pain. It hurt like hell. My parents took me over to see a doctor approximately fifty kilometers away from our home. My mom called his office in advance to let him know we were coming and what happened. The doctor took a look at my wounds, disinfected them, gave me a few stitches, and a tetanus shot. He didn't have a very good bedside manner; before we left, he gave me some antibiotics and told my mom the next time we disturbed him from his afternoon fishing, it had better be for something a little more serious.

Chapter 4

At the end of that school year, there was a girl I was particularly attracted to. Her name was Renée. We promised we would continue to see each other during the summer vacation. About a week after school finished for the summer, Renée called me. She invited my little brother and I to a party held at the house of one of her friends. They lived in the same little village where I went to school fifteen kilometers from our house. It was a problem because I knew my mother would never let us go but we decided to go anyway. The night of the party, we told my mom we were going to sleep in Guy's shack.

Guy, Bruce, and I hitchhiked down to the party. It didn't take us long to get a ride. A young woman stopped to pick us up. She knew Guy. She drove a sports car. She asked where we were heading and Guy told her the truth. She also asked how we planned to get back home. We told her we were leaving the same way. She was cool. She drove us right to where we needed to go; before dropping us off, she gave ten dollars to Guy and told us to get a taxi back. She said by the time we returned home, it would be hard to hitch a ride and she felt a little responsible for us since she brought us and she would never forgive herself if anything happened to us.

The party was lively and Renée looked amazing. We had a good time. I spent most of the time making out with Renée in the dark away from everybody. Her lips were warm and inviting. I'm sure I wasn't the first boy she kissed; by the end of the party, I was hooked. I didn't want to leave her. I could have stayed there all night; unfortunately, it was getting late and we had to go. Before leaving, Renée asked me if I would come back to see her soon. I told her I would because I believed I was in love.

To go back, we decided to try our hand at hitchhiking again. We gave ourselves a time limit of fifteen minutes, and if by then we didn't get a ride, we would take a taxi. We were almost ready to give up, when a vehicle stopped to pick us up. Bruce and I got in the backseat. Guy sat in the front with the driver. He seemed like a pleasant fellow, until he asked if we would like to make some money. Guy asked how and he said by letting him touch our private parts. I was shocked and disgusted by his request, but Guy spoke up right away and told him no way. Guy also said he was a pig and he'd better leave us alone. The man said, "OK. OK. I'll leave you alone." The rest of the ride back went smoothly but I was eager to get out of the car; that man gave me the creeps.

He dropped us off a short while afterwards in front of Guy's house. We were relieved to get out of there and it wasn't a moment too soon. We headed home after saying goodnight to Guy. On our walk back, we talked about Guy and how he handled himself with that dirty old man. He was brave for a little guy. I don't know what my reaction would have been if he hadn't spoken up. I admired him for the way he kept his cool. When we got home, we snuck back in the house undetected and headed straight to bed.

The next morning, our mom asked why we came back home to sleep. We told her the mosquitoes were eating us alive and we preferred to return home to sleep in our cozy bed.

The very next day, I was already devising a way to get back to see Renée. On the following Friday, I told my mother I was spending the night over at Guy's house. We had it all figured out.

Guy knew someone who was going where we needed to go. We arranged for them to pick us up at the restaurant where Guy's sister, Melissa, was working. I got there a little bit earlier and I was happy to see Melissa was serving behind the counter. I took advantage of the moment to sit at the counter and order a drink so I could see and talk to her. It was nice; I hadn't seen her practically all winter.

Guy arrived shortly after. I didn't even have time to finish my drink because we had to go; although, before leaving, I asked Guy in front of his sister how come he was so ugly and his sister was so pretty. Melissa got a good laugh out of that but Guy didn't think it was funny. He punched me on the shoulder and told me to hurry up. Our ride was waiting outside the door.

When we arrived, Renée was there waiting with friends. The weather that evening was perfect. It was warm and there wasn't a cloud in the sky. Renée knew of a quiet place where we could go to be alone and undetected. She took me to a large open field that wasn't too far. It was just perfect because we could lie down in the tall grass without being seen. The time went by so fast, before we knew, it was time to leave. We hitchhiked back. We were lucky because we got a ride right away with someone we knew. When we got to Guy's house, Melissa was sitting at the kitchen table having a late night snack. I was glad to see her there. We sat down with her and Guy made us something to eat. We stayed up talking for over one hour. Melissa was the first one to go to bed, and Guy and I went shortly after.

The next morning Melissa made breakfast for everyone. She was really a sweet girl. After we ate, I offered to help Melissa do the dishes and she accepted. We were both beginning to feel comfortable with each other. I liked the fact we could be friends. I liked being around her but I never expected anything more from her than friendship, even though, deep down I wished at times it could be more. But I knew it could never be because she was a little older than I and she was interested in older boys.

Two weeks later, Renée invited Guy, my little brother, and I to a party at her house. We hitchhiked down again. The party was great. We were having a really good time when suddenly, we heard a knock on the door. It was my mother and she wasn't happy. We had to leave right away. We didn't even have time to say a proper goodbye. It was the last time I ever saw Renée. We moved away on the very next day but I managed to persuade my parents to stop on the way at Guy's house, so we could say our goodbyes. It was devastating. I loved the people and area, but I was going to miss, Renée, Guy, and his family.

I will always cherish those memories of the good times I had with my best friend, Guy, and all the people I grew close to. I would miss Renée, in particular, because I was in love with her. I thought when I was with Carole, I was in love but I wasn't really. I was more in lust. With Renée, it was different. I was truly in love and here I was leaving her without any notice. I didn't even get the chance to kiss her goodbye. I tried to console myself by telling myself it was probably better I not see her because I hated to say goodbye. The pain would be too overwhelming.

Chapter 5

Our new home was nothing compared to our previous one. It had a small laneway and a little backyard. The house wasn't big; it was a three-bedroom bungalow with an unfinished basement. We spent the remainder of the summer renewing old acquaintances; it didn't take long before I had a whole new circle of friends.

We received some unexpected news that fall. We were being sued by the father of my little buddy who was with my brother and me when we had our skidoo accident. We discovered we weren't the only one; Carole's brother was also being sued by the father of my little friend. On our lawyer's advice, we decided it would be preferable to launch a lawsuit against Carole's brother to help pay for the monetary damages we were to incur if we lost our case.

We went to court that summer; it was strange to see everyone there. There was Carole, her sister, and brother of course. There was also my little buddy and his dad. I didn't have the chance to speak to anyone because we were advised by our lawyer not to talk to anybody before the outcome of our case. Bruce and I were asked to give our testimony of the event that happened on the night of the accident. We both felt nervous and intimidated. Nevertheless, we did what we were told, which was to tell the truth the way we experienced everything and to answer the questions to the best of our knowledge. The outcome wasn't as good as we expected it to be.

In the end, we lost our case. The court informed us that we would pay for half the damages and that Carole's brother would assume the other half. It was hard to take.

September arrived; I wasn't looking forward to going back to school. My first day was nerve-racking. We had to walk to school about two kilometers away from our home. I found walking such a long distance to be extremely tiring. I also had to adapt myself again to a whole new environment but luckily the school wasn't too big. It only had one floor, with one long corridor and a gymnasium that also served as a lunchroom; it wasn't too strenuous for me to get around.

I quickly made friends with some of my classmates. The school year went okay. I managed to pull through, despite all my difficulties: vision, coordination, and walking.

My parents decided we were going to build a house, and our good friends and past neighbors would do the same. Our two families bought a property next to each other. The plan was to get the foundation, framework, and plumbing done and we would do the rest. Our friend was a good carpenter and my dad knew electricity.

We spent most of the summer vacation working on both houses. Unfortunately, fall arrived and our house was far from complete. It meant we couldn't move in before school started. It was a disappointment but we had to make do.

I began high school that year, which meant I had to adapt myself again. The school was huge compared to what I was used to. My first day of school was completely overwhelming! It was an orientation day. We were instructed to meet in the cafeteria in order for us to get our schedule so we could begin our day. It was complete mayhem. We waited in line for over an hour to pick up our schedule. When I received it, I realized I was in trouble because the paper the schedule was written on was a light green. The print was very small, and it was a light blue and black. It made it impossible for me to see anything. Panic struck. I couldn't see where I was supposed to go. I tried to seek out a familiar face: someone I could show my schedule to and see if they had the same one as me. I got lucky. I came across a group of my old classmates and discovered two of them had the same schedule as I. It was a relief because all I needed to do was follow them to find out where I had to go.

It was a stressful day. Nothing went right. The building had two stories and a basement; to get between each floor, there was a flight of stairs that had sixteen steps. There was no elevator and I would have to change floors several times during the day in between classes. Each one of my classes was at different ends of the corridor and the numbers of every door were written on the top frame in print too small for me to distinguish. I had to count and memorize each door where every one of my classrooms was. When I entered my class, I discovered, to my dismay, that the blackboard wasn't black. It was green and I couldn't really see anything written on it. There was simply not enough contrast between the white of the chalk and the green of the board. As if that wasn't enough, we were each assigned a locker with a numbered lock. There were hundreds of lockers. Row upon row; it made it extremely hard for me to locate my locker. I was having a very difficult time decoding the numbers on my lock. I was in trouble. Everything was against me.

My first couple of weeks were hard. Certain subjects like mathematics and French were difficult. I was having trouble getting to and from my classes because we only had ten minutes to commute in between and most of my classes were scattered from one end of the school to the other. It was exhausting for me to have to go to my locker after one class and to get my books for the next. It was too much. I just couldn't do it on time and half the time, once I got to my locker, I couldn't get it open so I just gave up. I came to the conclusion that it would be simpler if I brought everything home and carried with me the material I needed for the day. So, I carried my books and other material around with me everywhere I went. It was a nuisance but I had no choice because it was all I could do. It was tiring to have to haul those things everywhere.

High school was a completely different environment when it came to teaching. The class was filled with students and the teachers didn't have time for any lengthy explanations. They really didn't care if we attended class or not. It was entirely up to us.

We moved into our new house on December twenty-third, 1973, two days before Christmas. It wasn't an easy task because we were located in an open field. There was no real road to get to the house, and we had to walk in snow two or three feet deep. There was about sixty-five meters to get from the road to the house. It was a difficult time but we were glad to finally be in our new home. The house wasn't entirely finished. It had a few touch-ups to do but all the essentials were done. We put the Christmas tree up on Christmas Eve. Bruce enjoyed doing the decorations; it was kind of a tradition. It was a memorable Christmas. We spent our time with our neighbors and friends, celebrating the holiday season in the comfort of our new home.

The house was built on a hill. Our backyard faced the rear of my high school. In order for me to get to school, I had to go down a fairly long, steep hill. At the bottom, I needed to go up another very steep slope to reach the backyard of the school. Once on level ground, I had to walk up thirty-two steps to reach the top of the balcony that led me into the school. It was a hard and tiresome thing for me to have to do every day, four times a day. I also had to deal with the long school corridors and the sixteen steps between each floor, along with my heavy school bag that I carried everywhere.

My legs, ankles, hands, and eyes were continuously getting weaker. Things were difficult. I often fell, going to or from school, or anywhere the terrain wasn't even, or in places that were slippery because of ice, snow, or loose gravel. My studies were impossible. I could no longer see what was written in my books. I occasionally took down notes in class, but when it came to reviewing them, I couldn't see what I wrote, so it wasn't of any help. Everything was stressful. I tried to keep all my anxieties, fears, and doubts inside. I didn't honestly believe anyone would understand what I was going through. It was difficult because I tried so hard to be normal. I kept saying to myself I was tough and I could take whatever came my way.

My first year of high school finally ended and I managed to get by without any failures. I don't know how. It was such a relief to be out of school. I looked forward to spending the summer vacation with my friends, camping and fishing. One of my buddies' parents had a piece of propriety on the side of a lake that was otherwise isolated. We enjoyed spending time there roughing it. My buddies were good with me because they knew I had a lot more difficulty getting around and doing certain things like walking, transporting heavy objects, and preparing and baiting my fishing line. They didn't hesitate giving me a hand, but I was stubborn and tried hard to carry the load.

I wanted to be as independent as everyone else. I often fell because of bad terrain: the rocks, tree stumps, branches, etc. Whenever it happened, I got right back up, gathered my things, and kept going. It happened to me fairly frequently but I never let it get me down. I was also quite small compared to my friends. My body wasn't developing normally. I was skinny, and no matter how hard I tried to get into shape by exercising, eating well, and doing weights. Nothing seemed to help. My muscles were simply not developing; it was an aspect of my condition I found hard to accept. I was having more problems with my lower limbs. My feet became high arched and turned inwards. My ankles were getting weaker too.

The first summer in our house was comfortable. We still had a lot of work to do behind the house, where there was a steep gully. We had to bring in much earth to fill in part of it to create a beautiful landscape. It was quite a heavy job! I helped a little by shoveling soil. The rest of my time that summer was mostly filled with my friends by fishing, camping, and simply hanging out. I went to stay with my grandparents for a couple of weeks. I always enjoyed visiting them. They owned a general store and every time I went down to visit, my grandfather let me work there. He had me doing everything from the inventory, restocking the shelves, cutting the meat, and working at the cash register. I just loved to work in the store! Most of the people who came in to buy were friendly and familiar faces, and I enjoyed fraternizing with them.

I occasionally took the afternoon off to go swimming with my cousins and friends in the river. There were two areas in particular we liked to go. One was a small beach close to town. It had a dock and a tug-boat docked there. We would dive or jump off the boat into the river. The water at that location was dirty. There was, at times, oil and diesel fuel leaking from the old boat. It wasn't sanitary at all, but we didn't mind because we were young and without fear. I injured myself there jumping off the back of the boat. Once I hit the water, my feet touched the bottom and I cut the sole of my right foot on a piece of glass from a broken bottle. After that incident, I stopped swimming there because I didn't trust the water.

The other area where we swam was the white bridge. It crossed the river on the main highway on the outskirts of town. Below the bridge, there was a nice, sandy beach, and people went there to swim and sunbathe. It was a popular place to go. Some of us occasionally jumped off from the edge of the bridge into the moving water below.

It was risky because at that time, it was common practice to transport logs by the river to the saw mills. There were always a few logs left over from the spring drive, and the odd log would somehow get snagged somewhere along the way. Eventually it got dislodged. We had to constantly be on the lookout for oncoming logs before taking the plunge. We had to be careful where we would dive. In certain areas of the river, there were dead ends, with logs stuck beneath the surface. We didn't really know where some of them were located, or how deep below the surface they were, but we were young and invincible. We were unaware of the imminent danger surrounding our careless acts. We were lucky; God was on our side.

I was sixteen years old and starting my second year of high school. I could no longer see to read. My hands and fingers were so weak, I could hardly do certain simple tasks like tying my shoes, buttoning my shirt or pants, and zipping my jacket or lapel. I didn't have enough strength and coordination in my hands to do any fine movements. My legs, feet, and ankles were losing a lot of strength. It was difficult keeping my balance while walking.

School that year was a nightmare. Walking and carrying my books with me everywhere became much more difficult. My body wasn't adapting well to the different temperature changes—especially my hands. Whenever I came in from the cold, if my hands were the least bit exposed to the frigid temperature, it took me a while before I could move them. It was inconvenient at times. I occasionally came in from the cold with a strong urge to void, and I would rush to remove my jacket and boots to make it to the toilet on time, but because of the weakness in my hands, it was impossible for me to do anything fast. It was often touch and go. Unfortunately, at certain times, I ended up getting wet. Whenever it happened, I tried hard to hide it. I didn't want anyone to know. It was too embarrassing.

During that winter, my feet and ankles were worse than ever. I was constantly twisting them and falling. I decided along with my parents to consult a specialist to see what he could do to correct the problem. After looking at several possibilities, with the advice of the doctor, we decided that I would undergo a surgery which involved stretching out the tendons in my feet to see if it fixed my deformity. I wanted to wait until my summer vacation to have the procedure done.

I spent the remainder of that winter trying to keep up with my studies. It wasn't easy. I got so tired of the whole situation, I just wanted it to stop. Every day for me became a constant battle. School was really hard and stressful. There wasn't a day I didn't fall for one reason or another. The constant walking, and going up and down the multitude of steps, was draining all my energy. I could no longer achieve anything productive. I just didn't see the purpose of continuing my studies.

One incident in particular was instrumental to my quitting; I was walking down the corridor one day and a group of students looked at me and began to laugh. I could hear them say to each other, "Look at him. He's drunk. He's walking all crooked."

I went by without saying a thing but it hurt. If only they knew how much I struggled every day to get things done! I tried hard to fight back the tears, but once I was out of the school and away from everyone's view, I cried all the way back home. After that incident, I quit. Every morning, I got up and pretended I went to school but I didn't go. My parents usually left to go to work before us kids went to school, so it was easy for me to stay behind without them suspecting a thing.

Summer vacation finally arrived and I went in to the hospital as planned to get operated on both feet. I was somewhat apprehensive but if it was going to correct my walk, I had to go through it. The night following my surgery, I was in a lot of pain. It was hot and muggy. The hospital was old and it didn't have any air-conditioning.

I had both my legs propped up onto pillows and in a cast up to my knees. The blood was seeping through and it was painful. I was hot and sweaty and totally uncomfortable. I pressed my call bell to see if I could get something to relieve the pain and help me sleep. A male nurse answered my call. I asked him if I could have some medication to feel better. He said he would have to check my medical chart to see what he could do. He returned shortly after and said he couldn't give me anything; I would have to wait another hour and a half before I could get medicated.

I was visibly disappointed, so he said, "Let me rub you down with rubbing alcohol. It will cool you down and you will feel better." I told him it would be nice. He raised the head of my bed and gently pulled me forward and slowly began to rub my back. It really felt good. The rubbing alcohol on my skin had a nice cooling effect. He asked if I liked it and I told him it was great. After he was done rubbing my back, he lowered the head of the bed, removed my hospital gown, and began rubbing my upper body, arms, chest, and belly. The coolness of the alcohol made me shiver. It gave me goose bumps. He started rubbing my legs but he was beginning to make me feel uncomfortable. He got too close to my private area and he spent too much time there. I started to get aroused and he began to fondle me. I told him to stop, but he didn't listen to me. He kept on and I told him to stop once again! He said, "Relax. It will make you feel a lot better," while at the same time he took a firm grip on my penis and continued to abuse me. I was in shock; I didn't know what to do. I froze and while he was abusing me I had mixed emotions: guilt and embarrassment, but at the same time what he did felt good and I didn't know how to react. I let go and surrendered to his abuse.

After, I was totally confused and ashamed. That incident really had me questioning myself. Why did I let him do that to me and why didn't I insist he stop? What he did was wrong and I should not have let him do it; but the truth was once he began, the feeling was too overpowering and I couldn't resist. That incident haunted me for many years. The following day, the doctor came by and asked how I was doing. I told him I was fine and I was ready to go home. I was in tremendous pain; I tried not to let it show because I didn't want to spend another night with that male nurse. The doctor said he would prefer it if I stayed another night. I asked why. He told me he would rather keep me there for observation, in case there were any complications. I answered him, pleading that I felt well and I would be much better off at home.

It was way too hot and muggy inside the hospital to have any comfort. The doctor said if I could put both my legs down, on the side of the bed, and if I managed to put weight onto my feet, he would let me go home. I did so but the pain was excruciating. I was shaking and dripping with sweat.

Still I was given permission to go home. I don't know what I would have done if I had to stay there one more night. I didn't want to see that man again because I was so ashamed by what he did to me.

The rest of the summer was a little tough because it was a hot year, and with both my legs in a cast, it was hard, although, it didn't stop me from doing a lot of my normal activities. I had two walking casts on, which made it a little bit easier to get around. I could still ride a bicycle, walk short distances without crutches, and occasionally, go camping and fishing with my buddies. They were always good to me. They helped by taking on most of the load. Whenever they saw me struggling, they gave me a hand.

I went as usual to visit my grandparents, uncles, and cousins. I always enjoyed those visits. That summer in particular was more difficult. With both my feet in a cast, I couldn't swim, and whenever my cousins and friends went for a dip, I could only sit by and watch. But despite certain inconveniences, the summer was good.

I wasn't looking forward once again to going back to school. I no longer had the motivation or the strength to go, and I didn't see the purpose in resuming my studies. I was depressed, tired, and discouraged but I couldn't stay at home and do nothing; my parents and I had a talk with the principal of the school and came to a compromise. In order to prevent me from staying at home and becoming too isolated, we agreed that I could go to school whenever I liked, and attend the arts and crafts class. It helped me to cope a little with my situation. The professor was nice and accommodating. I was always welcomed in his class. I went almost every day and I didn't have a specific time to go, but the professor always took the time to attend to my needs. I created things made out of clay. I enjoyed working with the clay and making my own creations. I wasn't good at it but I occasionally came out with something nice.

I finally got both my casts off in mid-October. What a relief. It was painful to walk around for the first month. It was mostly my ankles that gave me problems. Whenever I bent my feet to walk, the pain was excruciating. I fell a lot during that first month because the terrain outside was wet with ice, slush, and snow.

During the evenings, I spent a lot of my time at our neighbor's house, playing cards with my friend David, until the late hours of the night. We also listened to the late night mystery shows broadcast on the radio. I didn't go home to bed until three or four o'clock in the morning. It was fun; I liked spending time with David. He was a cool guy.

One day after the holiday season, a couple of my friends persuaded me to go with them on a snowmobile excursion to a small bar, approximately twenty kilometers away in the bush. It took a little convincing but I went despite my numerous apprehensions.

The trip there was good. We arrived at the bar around six o'clock in the evening. It was nice to finally be in a warm and cozy place. We spent the evening there playing pool and having a drink. I couldn't drink too much because of my weak bladder. Whenever I drank alcohol, I had trouble remaining continent. My buddies, on the other hand, didn't have any problem with drinking whatsoever. The guy I was riding with started to feel no pain, and I didn't like the condition he was in. I convinced him that we should be going because it was getting late and we had a long way to go before we got back home.

On our return, the weather was much better. The wind died down and it wasn't quite so cold. It was a nice ride but my buddies were going a little too fast for our own good. I was sitting in the back in between my friend and the back rest, when suddenly we came to a sharp left turn and the snowmobile was going too rapidly to stay on track. When the driver tried to negotiate the curb, the back of the vehicle swerved toward the right and smashed against a large tree. My leg got crushed and I was immediately thrown from the vehicle, on the middle of the trail. My buddies didn't even notice my absence. They kept on going without a care in the world.

There I was lying in the middle of the trail, hearing the sound of snowmobiles echoing out into the distance. I wasn't sure in which direction they were coming from or how far they were. It was scary; I was in a vulnerable situation. With the sound of the snowmobile engines roaring from every direction, I didn't know if, or when, a snowmobile would come around the corner and run me over.

I was in agonizing pain. I knew my leg was broken but what hurt the most on impact was that a branch of the tree entered the right side of my groin. It was the first thing I felt and it hurt! There I was in the dark, in the middle of nowhere, waiting for my buddies to realize I was missing and to come back and get me. Finally, after a while, I heard the sound of snowmobiles getting close. I was hoping and praying it was my friends and not some other snowmobile rounding the corner to run me over. Thank God, it wasn't so. It was my buddies and I was happy to see them. They didn't quite believe me when I told them my leg was broken, but nevertheless one of my friends stabilized my leg with his boot laces and a couple of branches he cut from a nearby tree.

The ride back was painful. Every bump we came to in the trail made my leg jump. It gave me a lot of discomfort. My buddy was driving too fast. He didn't spare me any pain; he was in such a hurry to get me back he wasn't paying attention to what he was doing. He flew past every tree and branch along the way. He positioned my leg in a way that the major portion of it was sticking out of the snowmobile, and every time he raced close by a tree or its branches, I prayed my leg didn't get hooked on either one of them.

We finally arrived at an open road and, after travelling a couple of miles, we came to a little house. We could see there was a dim light inside; and there was a lot of smoke coming out of the chimney. We decided, after a little hesitation, to knock on the door to see if we could use their telephone, so that we could get some help. My buddies were still not quite persuaded my leg was fractured, and because of that, they were shy to knock on the door. They did anyway. The person who answered the door was nice. We explained the situation to him and he invited us in. One of my buddies called his dad and he came right away.

When I arrived at the hospital emergency room, they took me in quick. The nurses removed most of my clothing. It wasn't easy. They had to cut it off to get to my leg and the entire process hurt. The damage caused by the impact was plain to see. My leg was swollen. A branch perforated my calf and another dug into my groin. I was bleeding from both sites. They brought me over to the radiology department to get an x-ray. It wasn't a pleasant experience. I was dripping with sweat. The pain was so intense, I thought for sure I would pass out. They took me back to the emergency area to wait for the doctor to examine me. He arrived shortly after and informed my mom and me I needed to be transferred over to another hospital in order to get my leg repaired. The damage I had incurred was much too severe for them to do anything. They took me to a nearby hospital where I waited a long time before being seen by anyone. I was finally examined by a physician on call and he informed me that I needed to have a surgical intervention to repair the injury. They put me in a private room while I waited for my operation.

The night was long and painful. They put a temporary cast on my leg until I could get my surgery. My leg swelled so much during the night that the toes on my foot were swollen and blue. The pain was so intense the medication they gave me for pain and sleep didn't help. I couldn't sleep a wink. A nurse came by to evaluate my condition, and observed that my leg was much too swollen; I needed some relief. She got someone from the plaster room to cut my cast to give room for my leg to swell, without constricting the area, and causing a potential risk for a blood clot or even amputation. The cutting of the cast helped a lot. I was able to catch a few winks afterwards.

The operation was performed later that afternoon and everything went well. I was able to return home on the next day. They put a cast on my leg, halfway up my thigh for the first month. After, I was able to get by with a walking cast that went below my knee.

The remainder of the winter proceeded without a problem. I spent the majority of it in a cast. There wasn't much for me to do. I passed a lot of time with my neighbors, playing cards or watching television. I also spent time listening and recording music. I still had my faithful companion, Blacky. It sometimes got lonely and boring to stay at home alone with nothing productive to do, but luckily, my dog was there to talk to and give me a little warmth and attention.

My grandfather died that fall. It was sad for everyone, especially for me, because I could no longer work during the summer at the general store, doing the inventory, filling shelves, working the cash register and various other things. It was something I would surely miss. With the passage of my grandfather, my grandmother sold the store. My days working at the store were officially over.

My grandfather was a good man. Whenever anyone needed help, he didn't hesitate giving a hand to people down on their luck for one reason or another.

He did the same for his grandchildren. Whatever we wanted, we got. During the winter, he always sent us children a package full of treats.

He was quite the character and he had several vices. He suffered from alcoholism and every couple of years someone sent him away by ambulance to the nearest hospital for detoxification. In between those bouts, he compensated by taking a lot of narcotics. He loved to gamble. Even though it was illegal, the police kept it quiet and never did anything to interrupt a poker match. Everything for my grandfather was an addiction; he passed away drunk and stoned. It was never officially divulged that he died of an overdose of alcohol and narcotics. He constantly battled his demons; despite his addictions, he was a very good man.

Chapter 6

I began having more trouble with my walking and coordination. The operation I previously went through to correct the deformity in my feet hadn't helped at all. I consulted with another doctor; I had to wear braces on both my lower limbs to see if it kept my ankles straight to prevent me from constantly falling. It was a pain. They were uncomfortable, very hard for me to put on and off, and they weren't helping much. They were more of a hassle than they were worth. After spending a long, grueling summer with those braces, I decided along with my parents to consult another doctor. He suggested I undergo an operation that consisted of breaking some of the bones in my feet and ankles, and fusing them together. I underwent my first surgery with that doctor the next fall. I thought that my previous operations were painful, but they were nothing in comparison to this.

I spent all that summer with my right foot in a walking cast but it wasn't so bad. I was getting used to it. It became the norm for me. It didn't stop me from doing a lot of things with my friends, like fishing, or camping, and other things. Even though it wasn't easy with my foot in a cast, and with my progressive disease I, nevertheless, tried my best to remain as active as possible Luckily, my buddies were there to lend me a helping hand. I got my cast off my right foot that fall and the operation turned out well.

That winter, we went to visit my grandmother at her new home. We brought Blacky with us because he wasn't any trouble. The night before we left to return home, I let Blacky outdoors before retiring for the night. We waited for him to scratch on the door to come in but he didn't; we knew that there was something definitely wrong because it wasn't normal that he would stay out so long. We all went out looking for him that night but we couldn't find him; we had to return home that cold January day without my faithful and dear companion. We were downhearted; he would be missed by all of us.

Blacky was old and blind. My father had a theory; maybe he went wandering onto the nearby river, and fell in the water and drowned, or he simply felt too old and sore that he preferred to wander away in the forest to die.

The remainder of that winter season was long and boring. I no longer had Blacky. During most weekends, my friends, brothers, and I got together to have a poker game. More often than not, we played at my house because it was more convenient for me. It was a rough period because I had a hard time with my walking, vision, and hand coordination; it was difficult to play cards. Everything I wanted to do became harder, but my friends understood and assisted when I needed it. I was careful not to drink too much, especially alcohol, because I would constantly have to run to the toilet and it was something I could no longer do on my own. I was having trouble to unbutton my pants and even tying my shoelaces. I had to eventually come up with better solutions. My remedy was to change my wardrobe. I started to wear clothes that didn't have any fastenings and footwear with Velcro because it was easier.

I had to have an operation on my left foot the following summer, and I wasn't looking forward to it because of what I had previously gone through with my right foot. What I feared most was to have the pins that were keeping my bones fused together removed. It was done at my first cast change, right there in the plaster room. The pins were sticking out of my foot about a quarter of an inch; to remove them the doctor came with a set of pliers and yanked them out. It was a painful procedure and I dreaded going through that again, but it was something I needed to endure to improve my walking.

I spent all summer in a cast, so I couldn't do much of anything. I got it removed for good in the fall but the operation didn't go as well as my previous one. The results were disappointing. My foot remained twisted and that made it difficult for me to walk. The doctor gave me the option to have corrective surgery but I refused because I didn't want to go through everything once again. I'd had enough with doctors, casts, and hospitals.

That winter was long and boring; except for the odd poker game with my friends, there wasn't much to do. I got depressed and I was losing the capacity to function on my own; no matter how much I tried to improve my condition, things were getting worse. Everything I did was an effort. I came to the conclusion I would work at finding ways to save my energy, instead of trying to do certain tasks that were too difficult.

By the following summer, despite my operations, I couldn't walk without falling; I began to use a cane. It helped to keep my balance. I also bought myself a little motor scooter. It gave me much more freedom and independence. I could finally come and go without having to worry about how I got there.

My eyesight wasn't good. I had to constantly be aware of my surroundings. I relied a lot on my sense of hearing to get by because it was one of my senses not affected by my illness; my sense of taste and smell were also intact. That summer went by much too fast. I had to put my motor scooter away for the winter. It meant my freedom was gone. I became confined indoors with music and TV. I enjoyed going to my friends' homes since that gave me the opportunity to get out of mine, even though it was an inconvenience for me. I had to get dressed, deal with the bad weather, and everything it implied, such as icy terrain, inaccessible units, and difficulty getting to the bathroom on my own.

My strength and balance got worse, and the cane no longer helped me. I had to use crutches. I wasn't comfortable with them, but I reached the point where I couldn't do without them. I hated that! I considered it a big failure every time I had to give up something because I couldn't do it anymore, yet I had no choice but to accept things the way they were.

We had a misfortune that spring. I was outside at my neighbor's house, in the backyard, talking to my buddy, when my little brother Bruce arrived from school. When he opened the door, he yelled that the house was on fire. My first thought was the beeping I was hearing wasn't the alarm from the trucks signaling at the nearby construction site, but it was the house fire alarm and I should have realized it.

I called my mother at work to give her the bad news. It wasn't easy. It was the hardest thing I had to do. My parents worked hard at building our home and all of a sudden everything was up in smoke. I told my mom what was happening and she came right away to witness the damage. It hurt because we lost everything. We were discouraged. We didn't know what to do but we couldn't give up. We had no choice but to go on. There we were, all of a sudden with nowhere to go, so we rented a motel nearby to spend the night. The next day we needed to get organized. My parents sent me to stay at my aunt's house in Fort Coulonge until we could get some alternative living arrangements. Bruce and my parents stayed in our trailer until our house was rebuilt. My older brother, Chuck, had a place of his own then, so we didn't have to worry about him.

That summer at my aunt's was the best I ever had. My aunt, uncle, and cousins were just wonderful. I loved them all very much. They were like a second family to me. I also had many friends and we had fun together.

This occurred while Saturday Night Fever and the movie Grease came out. We did parties two or three times a week. We got together a group of guys and girls, and danced the night away, trying to imitate the moves of John Travolta and Olivia Newton John, although, because of my illness, I had a difficult time. My arms and legs were too weak to keep up with my buddies. Nevertheless, I tried to fit in. Thanks to my friends, I could do so. They didn't make me feel any different and that's why I loved being with them.

I had also made a girlfriend that summer. It was nothing serious but it was fun while it lasted. She was the sister of a friend. She was pleasant but she didn't fit in with the same crowd as I; therefore, I saw her occasionally when I wasn't with my friends. It suited us both that way. I liked to spend time with her and the feeling was mutual. We were both content with getting together when the occasion presented itself.

The local Legion back home organized a party to raise funds to get the things we needed for our new home. A lot of my friends, cousins, and I went to the party. We all had a great time. There were a lot of people. It gave my buddies from home the opportunity to meet some of my friends and the cousins I had spent the summer with, and they hit it off really well. The summer was ending and it was time for me to go home. The house was built. My cousins and friends also had to go back home to start school. I was disappointed to see them go. They were a nice group of people. Unfortunately, the good times we shared were over, and somehow, I knew it would never be the same.

My friends and I slept in the basement that night. The next morning, we got up and my mother made us breakfast. My buddies left shortly but they said before leaving they would return in a few weeks for my birthday party.

As promised, my friends came to celebrate my eighteenth birthday. I was happy to see them again. The party was held at my buddy's house. There were many people who showed up. We had a good time.

There was a girl I started to see before I went away that summer. She came to the party and gave me a necklace with my zodiac sign made of fourteen karat gold. It was a generous gift but I felt uncomfortable receiving it. She shouldn't have spent her hard earned money on me. I was confused. I didn't quite understand why she liked me despite my disease. She was a nice girl but I didn't know how to react toward her. I liked her, but I was unsure because I could feel that my physical condition was getting worse and I didn't want to get too involved in case I got hurt. My self-esteem was low and I couldn't see how anyone in their right mind would want to start a romantic relationship with someone such as me. After the party, my friends stayed, once again, at my house and left the next day. It was truly good to see them. I didn't think they would come, but they did, and I was thankful for it. They were really a great group of friends.

After they left, I resumed my daily routine. It was quite boring at times. It consisted of occasionally going out with my buddies, spending time at my neighbor's playing cards, watching television, or listening to music.

My condition got worse every day but I tried my best not to let it show. I was lonely and depressed. I felt worthless. I couldn't do anything productive. I was a nuisance to everyone. I hated myself and the troubles I caused. Nevertheless, I decided to resume my relationship with the girl from the party despite my fears and anxieties. After all, I liked her and she liked me. I didn't know why but I needed the companionship.

She was good to me, even though I wasn't always nice to her. I loved her but I refused to get too attached. She, on the other hand, loved me like crazy. She always wanted to be with me. I found her to be too attached to me. She stuck like glue. I felt trapped at times. She was suffocating me! I would go out with my friends on certain occasions, come in late, and the first thing I knew she would sneak in the house and hop in bed with me. If I didn't pay attention to her, she cried and said I didn't love her. It wasn't true. I did love and care for her; but I simply didn't want to get too emotionally attached.

It was a troublesome time for me. I was contending with the many losses to my health, autonomy, and independence. Deep down inside, it was me I didn't like. I kept trying to push her away. I didn't feel like I was worth loving, and I feared that eventually she would realize it and leave me.

We stayed together for almost three years and she was extremely devoted. I really don't know how she put up with me for all that time. I thank her in many ways for the time that we had together and I'm sorry for the hardship I put her through. I was extremely selfish. I was only thinking of myself; I didn't take her feelings into consideration and that is something I regret. She finally left me because her family moved away. I liked her very much but it was better that our relationship end that way because my illness was really affecting me. I was beginning to lose a lot of my independence and I was too proud to let her see me as an invalid. I didn't want her to take pity on me because she certainly didn't deserve that. It was better for her to move on and find someone else to take good care of her.

After she left, I was empty. My condition was getting worse. Everything was exhausting. My friends came less frequently. They occasionally called to invite me out but I always declined the invitation; eventually they stopped coming and calling.

It was simply too difficult to go anywhere; if I was to go out, there were a number of things to worry about. Things that any normal person wouldn't. Like walking without falling, getting dressed or undressed, tying my footwear and going to the bathroom. Those were functions I couldn't do without some type of assistance. It bothered me tremendously. I didn't want to seek help from anyone. I was too proud and I preferred to remain alone at home so I could keep the autonomy I had left.

As time went by, my condition deteriorated; I struggled every day to keep my independence. What I feared the most was to lose it. I didn't want to rely on others to take care of me but no matter how hard I tried, the time came where I needed help. My hands were totally paralyzed and of no use. My legs got weaker and I could hardly support myself; I used crutches to walk. I couldn't bear the weight of my body.

It was a very low period. I made a lot of compromises to make my everyday life easier. I didn't want to rely on my family for certain tasks. For the first time, I needed outside help. I got a social worker. We discussed my condition and what I needed to improve my quality of life. I told him I needed help bathing but I was reluctant to have strangers invade my privacy. I said I wanted assistance with my daily tasks. He informed me he would refer me to the rehabilitation center and arrange to have someone help with my shower.

The first time someone came over to bathe me was quite the experience. It was two older women. It was humiliating for me. What I needed most was assistance in and out of the shower, but they were too old and had back problems. I had a shower bench I could sit on to wash, although, it took a lot of energy to get the job done. After it was over, I was completely played out. I could sense that my two ladies were very nervous; ironically, they were telling me to relax. It was obvious they didn't know how to react to me. They gave me the shower real quick and didn't do a good job at that. I suspected that they weren't used to having such a young client as they didn't go anywhere near my genital area, and I was too shy to ask them to do better.

After their visit, I called my social worker. I told him it was embarrassing enough to ask for aid and he would have to find me better workers or forget it. He said he would see to it that I had a better person to meet my needs. He asked if I would prefer to have a male bathe me. I told him I would prefer a woman. It was always my mother or a female babysitter who took care of me and it would be strange for me to have a man. But I would accept that as long as it was someone who could do the work to my satisfaction. He assured me he would find someone to my liking.

The next person my worker sent to assist me was a woman in her mid to late fifties. My first impression of her was one of fear and apprehension; even though she seemed very nice, I wasn't sure she could do the job.

In the beginning, we were both a little shy and awkward, but things went surprisingly well; even though it was the first time that we were together, she did everything to my satisfaction. After she was through, I felt clean. I was happy to have her and I looked forward to seeing her again.

She ended up spending a couple of months taking care of me. She came by three times a week. I liked her and I was comfortable with her; however, I was forced to let her go because I got admitted to the rehabilitation center to see if they could do anything to facilitate my life.

Chapter 7

I liked my stay at the rehab and I met a lot of nice people. There was a young fellow who was the same age as I. He was there because of an accident and we got along well. The rehab center was fairly new and the personnel were all nice. My days there were occupied. I was busy doing physiotherapy, occupational therapy, psychology, etc. Everything that could enable me to make my life easier; but during the evening it was quiet and there wasn't much to do. We sometimes found things to do like going out shopping, to restaurants, or music concerts, and occasionally, I got together with a few clients and played Trivial Pursuit. It was a game I enjoyed. I like the concept of learning and the camaraderie I shared with my opponents.

During my stay at the rehab, I acquired my first wheelchair. It was a big change; at first I didn't want to hear about it but in the end, everybody persuaded me it would be better if I had one. I was stubborn and I didn't like the fact that I needed a wheelchair to get around but I thought that in a way it would probably make things much easier. I would no longer have to deprive myself from going anywhere because of long distances, my fear of falling, and having to use those darn crutches. I was reluctant to use it but I found it was much more useful than what I envisioned. It was less exhausting and I wasn't so preoccupied about falling; I returned back home with my new wheelchair but my going back home was an adjustment; at the rehab I was surrounded by people and busy doing things all day long, but at home I was alone during the day. I had nothing to do to pass the time.

My physical condition was gradually getting worse. I had a hard time to walk and to support myself. My hands were useless and every task I undertook was strenuous and exhausting. I had reached the point where I had to rely more and more on my wheelchair to get around indoors and out.

I was bored to death having to stay most of the time inside the basement all alone. I was beginning to feel worthless, isolated, and like I was a big burden to everyone. I was angry at my condition that was rapidly deteriorating; no matter how hard I tried to keep my autonomy, I was losing it and I was scared.

I tried hard to keep my cool all the time; but the more I needed help, the more I became bitter and resentful toward the people I loved and cared about. I was too proud and I wanted to continue to do everything on my own; I considered myself a failure. I hated to have to ask for anything, and the more I did, the more I felt useless.

It went on that way for a good while; eventually, I had to return to the rehabilitation center because I was losing my remaining autonomy. During that period, they helped me to get a new wheelchair. The one I had became too heavy for me to push around. I could no longer walk with my crutches and I relied solely on my wheelchair. The rehab provided me with a much lighter chair and it made my movements a lot easier. They fitted me with a special splint to hold my utensils while eating. It made the process easier and it permitted me to remain virtually independent while feeding myself.

They looked at renovating the basement to make my life manageable. They helped to make the bathroom more accessible and put in an elevator, so I would have access to the outdoors. It took a while before everything was in place. Luckily, I received my new wheelchair.

I was feeling lost at the time; I had nothing to do. I was longing to learn but I had no means. I could hardly see and I couldn't use my hands for anything. I couldn't walk and I didn't know what I could do to keep my brain stimulated. Despite my fervent desire to learn, the odds were against me. What I could basically do was listen to television and radio to keep myself informed in the hope I could educate myself that way.

My newest equipment was finally installed and they did a good job. There were a few complications with the elevator in the beginning but they got everything sorted out. The renovations certainly made things a lot easier, enabling me to do a few more things for myself. It made it easier to take my shower and to go to the toilet without assistance. It helped me keep some of my independence.

As time went on, I was stuck in my basement. Even though I had a special light chair, I could hardly move it. My arms were much weaker, and doing things on my own left me tired and frustrated.

I was lonely and isolated. Everyone around me had a busy life. I would literally drag myself up from the basement on my behind to have supper with my family. It was often depressing. Everyone sat around the dinner table discussing the day. I rarely had anything to talk about since I was more or less confined to the basement, with nothing to do except deal with my situation.

It got impossible to propel my wheelchair. I went back to the rehabilitation center and was assessed for a power chair. They worried that my vision wasn't good enough. The chairs were powerful and they were concerned about my safety and the safety of others. I underwent a driver's test with my occupational therapist to see if it was possible for me to maneuver a powered chair. It was scary. She made me drive it through all kinds of obstacles indoors and out. It was fun and I did well for the first trial. I was hoping I could get one of my own. The occupational therapist didn't believe I would be able to get funding because of my poor vision, even though I proved I could do it. If I wanted to have one, we would have to find the money elsewhere. I was lucky because the company where my mother worked gave me the funding to purchase my first powered wheelchair. I was able to get fitted, and to get all the adjustments and familiarize myself with the chair before leaving. I no longer had to second guess myself because of the terrain. I could go anywhere I wanted to without the fear of being too tired to continue or that I didn't have the strength to get there and back.

The rehabilitation center was trying to adapt computers for the physically disabled. I was interested and I asked my occupational therapist if it was possible for me to use one. The technology wasn't advanced at the time and the functions were limited. The technicians adapted the keyboard in a way so I could use it. My hands were virtually useless, so they created a special device that fitted over the keyboard. It basically consisted of a very thick plastic that covered the keys. It was full of holes in the place of the touches; with that, they made a special splint in order for me to press the keys. They came up with a contraption that consisted of a splint fitted onto my right hand that permitted me to hold a stick to press the keys. It wasn't the ideal thing but it was the best they came up with.

It was a strenuous device to use and it was frustrating at times to access the keyboard; learning how to use all the computer functions was difficult. It was a lot for me to process but, in a way, I truly enjoyed it. It felt good to stimulate my brain. I left rehab with a whole new outlook.

As for the computer, I was referred to a non-profit organization that dealt only with people who had vision problems. I went to meet the person in charge of the computers to see if they would finance my computer system. The individual I met with on that day wasn't nice. He asked me questions about the computer and what it could do. It was a subject I knew little about at the time. It was a new part of technology. Before I left, he asked what I expected from the computer. It was a question that caught me by surprise. I wasn't sure at the time what it could do. I just got a small introduction on the one at the rehab and nothing more; I didn't quite know how to respond. I told him I wasn't sure because I didn't know all the possibilities. He bluntly answered I should come back and see him when I knew what I wanted. I was insulted and disappointed by his reply. I said to myself someday I would show him. I wasn't stupid and if given the chance I could certainly thrive.

I eventually got a computer. Unfortunately, the adaptations they did for me at the rehab didn't work well and I discovered my functions with the computer were limited. I was only able to play a few simple games and to do a little bit of writing. I wanted to do more.

I enjoyed my powered wheelchair. During the warm weather, I spent my time outdoors. It gave me the freedom to go wherever I wanted to within certain limits. I drove around the neighborhood, which I was familiar with because of my poor vision.

One of our neighbors had a little girl. Her name was Mary Lou. She was four years old when I first met her. I took a liking to her. I found her to be so sweet. She had long, brown hair, halfway down her back, a freckled face, big brown eyes, and two top front teeth missing. I just loved her to death. She often went riding with me sitting on my lap. She enjoyed going for excursions with me around the neighborhood. With one of her parents' permission, we would occasionally go to the nearby corner store and I bought us both a treat. When she saw me outside, she came running and we went for a stroll. I thought she was so cute and I enjoyed her company.

My parents bought a swimming pool that year and tried to make it accessible for me. It wasn't easy to do because the way our backyard was constructed; the landscape wasn't at all suited for me. The pool could only be situated near the end of our property, near a little creek that flowed through the yard. The terrain was wet and swampy, so there were many adjustments to do to the land before the pool went into place. It was at the base of a steep hill facing the rear of our house. The hill was made into two parts, like a giant stair step. The first slope was approximately twelve feet. Then, we arrived at a levelled area that was also around twelve feet. After doing so, we had to descend once more another steep slope that was similar to the previous one to get to the pool at the base.

It was an above ground pool and my dad constructed a little bridge that led on to the deck. He built a group of stairs to get from the top of the hill to the pool. I remember it well. Each set of stairs had eleven steps to go down and up; I journeyed those steps almost every day during the warm season. Whenever it was hot enough, I spent all my afternoons in the pool. The only way for me to reach the pool was on my bum. I dragged myself up and down those steps every time I went swimming. Luckily, I still had a little strength in my arms, or else I wouldn't have been able to go in the pool whenever I wanted. It was strenuous at times but I loved being in the water. The buoyancy of the water made it easy for me to maneuver around. I felt free in the pool because I could swim and walk without too much of an effort. The cooling of the water made me feel stronger, especially on those hot and muggy days.

I went on that way for the first two summers we had our swimming pool, but after that, I didn't have the strength. My father devised a contraption designed to facilitate my getting to and from the pool. It consisted more or less of a small wagon on wheels with a kind of wooden train track. It was attached to an electric winch that was secured at the top of the hill; from there, I got someone to sit me on the wagon and it lowered me down to the pool deck with a simple press of a remote control unit. Once on deck, there was a hydraulic lift attached to a chair and I transferred myself from the wagon onto the chair and the lift lowered me in the pool; to get out, it was the same process but only in reverse. It was practical and a lot less strenuous for everyone.

The summer season was great; there were a lot more things I could do. I liked to drive around the neighborhood with my wheelchair. I enjoyed going to visit people I knew in the surrounding area and to take some of the kids who were there for a ride on my lap with my powered chair. I loved all the children who were around but the one I cherished the most was my little, brown-eyed girl. I tried to be fair with everyone but she took priority. I taught her how to drive my chair and it didn't take her long before she was driving me all around the neighborhood. I sometimes had a problem because whenever my little niece came over to visit, the competition started. It was hard because I loved them both. They were both the same age, and I tried to be fair, but my little niece was totally jealous of Mary Lou. My little friend would understand and keep away when my niece came. I felt sorry for her, but I tried my best to make it up to her when my niece left.

The winter was long and dull after spending such a busy summer outdoors. I went from doing a lot to doing nothing, seeing many people to seeing nobody. I was confined in my basement all day with nothing better to do than watch television. It was something I didn't get pleasure from doing due to my poor vision. I couldn't distinguish the images on the screen, and as for the radio there wasn't much to listen to so I could educate myself. I got depressed about my condition. I didn't like the feeling. Due to my illness, I was losing my ability to take care of myself. My eyes were weak; I was at the stage where I could hardly see anything but certain shapes and colors. It depended on the extent of the lighting. The brighter the light, the harder it was to see. My hands lost all their strength; I could no longer walk and I could barely function on my own. I was angry and frustrated at my physical condition. I was trying to find some kind of outlet for my emotions. I felt like I was wasting away. My body was failing me, but my mind was still very bright and hungering to learn.

Suddenly, the answer came to me one afternoon while sitting in front of the television turning the channels, trying to find something interesting to listen to. I came across a documentary about a rehabilitation center in Montréal that specialized in adapting the computer for individuals with a physical disability. I said to myself, "This is it. This is what I was looking for."

I was excited. I took in the information needed to contact the center and called my mother at her office to write it down in case I forgot. The following day, I contacted the center in Montréal and they arranged for me to go there for an evaluation and interview to see if I qualified for their program. Three weeks later, I was on my way to Montréal with my parents. It was on a Monday early in the morning. We decided it was preferable if we went on Sunday and spent the night so we would be there on time.

We found a small Bed and Breakfast in proximity to the rehabilitation center. It was an old house that wasn't very wheelchair accessible. My mother and I stayed in one room and my father in another. The room I was in with my mom had a double bed. It was the only room that didn't have any steps so I could go inside. The bathroom was a different story. It had a step to go in and the doorway was too narrow for my wheelchair to go through, therefore,

I couldn't use it. It was a problem but it wasn't one that couldn't be overcome because luckily, I thought of bringing my urinal.

My mom cleaned me up in the morning with a facecloth. After doing so, we went to have a quick breakfast and hurried on to the rehab center to make it for eight thirty a.m.

When we arrived, we met with a woman by the name of Nellie; she invited me into her office, and proceeded to question me on various aspects of my life and physical condition.

My parents were not allowed to stay with us during the interview. We talked on various topics. Mostly about what I could do for myself — things like if I could bear weight, transfer, wash, dress, and feed myself. She wanted to know why I wanted to obtain their service. After she was done questioning me, it was my parents' turn to be interviewed and I wasn't allowed to stay while they were speaking. I felt nervous and apprehensive because I thought that I shouldn't be left out of the conversation since they were most likely talking about me and I was curious to know what they were saying.

Once the interviews were over, Nellie said she would contact us after she spoke with the members of her team to see if I was a good candidate for their program, and if they could do anything to improve my quality of life.

Approximately two weeks after returning home, I got a call from rehab to tell me that I was being admitted on the following Monday. The next Monday, as planned, we were on our way, once again, to Montréal. I was scared, not knowing what the future held in store. I was also excited at the prospect of learning something new.

Chapter 8

Upon my arrival at the rehabilitation center, I began to familiarize myself with my new environment. Due to my low vision, I relied on my other senses to orient myself. The rehab was located at a higher level than the street. We went up a very steep hill to enter the building. The doors were automatic and there were two sets to enter into the main lobby. The reception desk was on our left, past the second set of doors. I could tell because of the telephones ringing nonstop. The lobby was fairly wide and there was a set of elevators on the right, and a larger one facing them. Farther down, at the far end of the lobby, was the cafeteria. I could easily tell by the aroma and by the clinking of the dishes.

We took the single elevator to the third-floor, and upon our arrival, Nellie was there to greet us; she took me over to my room so I could unpack and acclimate myself to my new surroundings. After doing so, she brought me around to introduce me to a few of the residents.

So there I was: in Montréal, in completely strange and unfamiliar surroundings. I was a little scared but at the same time I was excited because I looked forward to the prospect of working with the computer: the instrument that would potentially enable me to read and write.

The unit where I was staying had a fairly big living room and kitchen. It was a common area where residents could meet, eat, watch television, or listen to music. It was also a place where we could go to relax. That's where I first met Henri. He was sitting at the table munching on cookies and milk. I sat beside him and introduced myself. He told me his name and that he was from Chile. I could tell right away he was a very nice person. He asked me if I knew his buddy Marc and I said I didn't. He told me Marc was his friend and I should meet him. As he spoke, a young man came wheeling in and Henri introduced him to me. It was Marc; he was a pleasant young man, approximately twenty-five years old, about the same age as Henri. We spent the rest of the afternoon getting acquainted.

The next day, Nellie took me over to meet my occupational therapist. Her name was Catherine; she was in her late forties. She was tall and slim with a professional attitude. She made a good first impression on me. I looked forward to working with her.

After discussing my needs, Nellie took me over to the computer lab and introduced me to the professor who was in charge. He was a big man with an engaging smile. Together, we discussed what they could come up with to help me reach my goals. By the time we were done talking, it was already lunchtime. We took a break but before leaving, we agreed that we should meet later on that afternoon so I could try out a few things.

I went for lunch in the cafeteria. I found the way everything was organized interesting. Residents, such as me, with very little mobility, had a meal helper. They followed them to the table of their choice and helped with whatever they needed to eat on their own. I used a special splint on my right hand to enable me to hold a spoon, so I could feed myself. They helped me put it on and removed it when I was done eating. Everyone there had a different way to function. The meal helpers were trained to work with people with various degrees of mobility, and to help with different kinds of apparatuses that helped the residents to maintain their independence as much as possible.

The cafeteria staff was extremely helpful. They were used to being around people with disabilities. I didn't sense any apprehension or intimidation from them by the way they interacted with the residents.

After lunch was over, I went up to my room to listen to music. I was lucky because I had a room by myself and I could do what I wanted. I found out that during the lunch hour, there wasn't any staff working on the floor. It wasn't convenient because I needed to go to the washroom and I required some assistance. On that particular day, I didn't have enough time to go during the morning and my bladder was full. I couldn't wait much longer but luckily, I had my music to distract me until I could get some assistance.

Nellie arrived early and helped me. Afterwards, we went to meet my physiotherapist. She was a nice young woman and I liked her right away. She was intrigued by my physical condition. She started to ask me the same questions I was asked many times before. She got me to transfer myself onto the exercise table to see how much mobility I had. She looked at my sensory perception by touching me in different areas. She had me move my arms and other parts to check my coordination. After we were finished, I returned to the computer lab to familiarize myself with the environment and to look at the various adaptations that were available.

I quickly adjusted to my new place. I enjoyed the atmosphere that surrounded my temporary home. The people were warm, friendly, and helpful. My first couple of months were spent trying to find the right adaptations to gain access to the computer. It took a while but finally we found something that could possibly work, thanks to the collaboration of the Louis Braille Institute. They found a good voice output in combination with a program made to use the Morse code. I was ready to embark on an exciting adventure. I spent most of my days learning how to operate the computer with my special programs. It wasn't easy at times; it was a course of trials and errors. I sometimes got so tired and discouraged, I felt like we would never find a way for me to use the computer. It often froze on me and I got frustrated; but with persistence, finally things started to pay off and I gained ground.

I was starting to feel at home in Montréal with my new friends. I knew the place from top to bottom, and everyone who worked there, and how everything was set up.

I began to get involved in the politics of the establishment by joining the residents' council. I found it interesting because it gave me some insight on how the organization functioned, where their funding was coming from, and how it was administered.

My days were mostly filled but my evenings weren't too occupied. There wasn't much to do. The rehab center had a swimming pool in one of its buildings across the street. It was a new building equipped with a large pool and a hot-tub. Marc, Henri, and I went to swim there twice a week, and two of our attendants accompanied us and helped. The rest of my evenings were mostly spent at the computer lab or in my room listening to music with Marc and Henri.

There was an attendant who worked there during the evening that I particularly liked. Her name was Annie. She was a tall, slim girl with light brown hair. She was so sweet and had a great sense of humor. She was a student working there to make ends meet. She was going to be an occupational therapist. I spent a lot of time sitting in the living room or kitchen talking with her and we became good friends. We sometimes went out to restaurants or took long walks together. I enjoyed every moment with her. She was just perfect and much too beautiful for someone like me. My self-esteem was very low at the time and I didn't think that anyone in their right mind would ever want to have someone like me. I basically gave up on girls altogether.

The third floor where I stayed was divided into two separate units; one side was allocated for a clientele of quadriplegics and paraplegics. The other side had people who suffered from different degenerative diseases. It was kind of like two separate cultures. The quadriplegics didn't like to mingle with people who had any other types of disabilities other than their own. Being disabled was something entirely new to them but eventually, with time, I figured they would come around. In a certain way, I sympathized with what they were going through because it mustn't have been easy having your life change so drastically in a matter of seconds due to an unfortunate accident. I couldn't help but feel sorry for them, even though I had problems of my own.

The majority of the quads were into substance abuse. They weren't handling their new life well. Some were heavily into cocaine and other types of hard drugs. Against all odds, we became friends. As mentioned before, I sometimes listened to music in my room and I liked it loud. Occasionally, a few of the quads crossed over to join me. We liked the same music — bands like Springsteen, Bon Jovi, and Phil Collins — and that's how I became friends with most of them. They were in a category of their own. They were wild but a nice bunch of fellows. I enjoyed spending time with the people living on both sides. On my side, there wasn't really anyone on the same cognitive level as I, but nevertheless I enjoyed spending time with them, especially Henri, Marc, and Pascal.

Pascal was a little guy who had muscular dystrophy, and he was quite the character. Those three were always making me laugh.

They were constantly getting into mischief. They were a group of sexually deprived, immature young men. All they talked and thought about were women and every female they saw was subject to their scrutiny.

I gave up on sex a while back because I found it to be too frustrating. I didn't think anybody would want to have anything to do with me, but after hanging around with those guys, I regained an interest. There were a couple of girls at rehab who were promiscuous. They liked boys a lot. Marc and Henri occasionally spent time with them.

One evening, I was alone in my room, listening to music, when one of the girls came knocking. She asked if she could come in; even though I was feeling uncomfortable having her there, I let her in. She was attractive and I didn't know how to react around her. After a while, she approached me and asked if I would like to kiss her. I could feel myself blushing but I awkwardly gave her a kiss. It felt good! I hadn't kissed a girl that way for a while. She wasn't shy and knew how to please me. She made me feel like I hadn't felt in a long time.

I had a few more similar encounters with her after that. I also had a few with her friend but I quickly got tired of them. I enjoyed my time with them, but they were just a little too immature for me. In a certain way, I kind of felt sorry for them because they believed that sex and love were something that went hand and hand, but it wasn't necessarily so; they were just a couple of young, lonely women who were looking for love and attention but instead they were being used. I was one of those who took advantage of their naivety for my own self-gratification. It's something I wasn't proud of, but they opened the door for me and I took advantage because I was curious; I wanted to see if I could still function sexually. They were there when I needed them and I am grateful for what they gave me.

There was a young woman on the quadriplegic side whom I befriended. Her name was Sandra she was a recent arrival. She also liked to play loud music and that's how I began to notice her. We had the same taste in music and we started to visit each other and soon became close friends. She introduced me to a few of her friends who were also quadriplegic. They were people who had a big chip on their shoulder because they had a hard time coping with their disabilities. They were at rehab to learn how to function with their limitations. Sandra was friends with a quad named Virgil. He was a big man who was very proud and didn't accept the condition he was in. He had a little movement in his right arm and could slightly move his head. But as for the rest, he was completely paralyzed. He was also the only person there who just spoke English. He was a stubborn and angry Englishman. He had no patience whatsoever and he wasn't easy to deal with. People had to be careful in the way they approached him but luckily, for my sake, he liked me. We used to get together, Sandra, Virgil, and I to play a game of Yummy or Trivia. We took the occasion to have a few beers to unwind.

If Virgil liked you, he was the kindest, nicest person in the world. I liked him a lot. He was a tough guy, I'm sure, before he had his accident; nobody messed with him. Deep down inside, he had a heart of gold but the saddest thing about Virgil was that he was too proud. He found it too difficult to be taken care of. Having strangers invade his intimacy was too embarrassing.

The majority of the quads were a good bunch of fellows. They all seemed to accept their fate but in various degrees. Some of them were better than others. It was easy to tell by their willingness to work hard at trying to rehabilitate themselves.

Things were quiet at the rehab center during the week but on the weekends it was often wild. There was always a party going on. It usually started on Friday evening and ended most of the time Sunday afternoon. There were a lot of booze and drugs going around. It was time to unwind and to get rid of some major frustrations that occurred during the week.

The attendants who worked there were cool. They liked to have a good time and join in on the party. The fun lasted until the early hours of the morning and the music blasted all night. Some of the guys occasionally got prostitutes to come and join the party to give them a good time. Others had their girlfriends over for the weekend. The only thing the administration asked was to advise the receptionist when they had a guest staying overnight for reasons of security; in case there was a fire, or any other type of disaster, they had to know how many people needed to be rescued.

There was one person there in particular who didn't accept, at all, his newfound disability. He was a young man in his early twenties. He couldn't deal with his condition, and took out his frustrations with drugs and alcohol and had no limits. He was rude and obnoxious most of the time, especially with the attendants. He treated them with disrespect, as though they were at his command. No one liked him. He only had one friend there who was a paraplegic. It was obvious they needed each other. Mr. Obnoxious used his friend to get drugs and alcohol to numb his pain, and his buddy would assist him to administer them. In turn, he got what he needed to support his own addictions.

One particular Saturday evening, I was in the sunroom on the quad side having a drink with my friends, when suddenly, Mr. Obnoxious came in and began to complain about everything. When he saw me there with my buddies, he rudely asked me what the hell I was doing in his sunroom. I had no business being there, and I should return on the other side, with the rest of the "retarded people."

I said to him, "What's your problem? Why do you have to be so obnoxious? You make me sick with your self-pity. Why don't you smarten up and accept the way you are? I wish I was in your shoes. You can get better, but instead, you're doing everything in your power to destroy what you have going for you."

The people there agreed with me, and told him to wake up and get a life. He became angry and left the room, telling us we were all crazy.

Shortly after that altercation, Mr. Obnoxious was asked to leave the rehab because he wasn't actively participating in his rehabilitation. He refused to co-operate with his therapists. He was clearly on a self-destructive path, and because of that, the rehab center no longer wanted to accommodate him in doing so. I wonder what became of him.

Things were moving along well with the computer. I finally achieved my goal to read and write and navigate on the screen. I knew exactly where the cursor was so I could work and see in my mind what I was writing. My next step was to get a new motorized wheelchair. The one I had was old and unreliable. My occupational therapist thought it was a good opportunity while I was at rehab. She got me to try out a few models, but I didn't like any of them, so I decided I would stick with the same model because it suited my needs. I found out, to my dismay, that the manufacturer was no longer making it. I reluctantly tried out their latest and I liked it. It drove much easier; I decided it was the chair for me. The following day, I went over with Catherine to get fitted. The building contained many professional departments. They had a big wheelchair repair shop and an occupational therapy department where they made all sorts of splints, prostheses, and many other adaptations to enable somebody to function better.

They also had various medical professions, a library, a volunteer department, a gymnasium, Jacuzzi, swimming pool, and a few other things to accommodate people with a physical disability.

I had a bad experience one night while in bed. I turned over to my right side and ended up falling on the floor. I hit my head on the dresser on the way down but despite my misfortune, I only got a little scrape on my forehead. Besides that, everything else was okay, although, the floor was so cold. I was lying there naked because I normally slept that way. I found it was less difficult for me to reposition myself in bed without clothes. If I wore pajamas, it restricted my ability to move, but that night, I wish I had worn my pajamas. I was lying on the floor in a very uncomfortable position and I could hardly move. My call bell was way out of reach and I had no way of calling for help. My room was the last one at the far end of the hallway. It was Friday night and the quads were having a party. There was no way to signal for anyone. Their parties usually lasted all night and the attendants stayed with them most of the time.

I was hoping someone, somehow, would come to my rescue, but it wasn't so. I tried to get myself closer to the door to bang on it, in the hope that someone would hear me but the floor was too slippery. I tried many ways but I simply couldn't do it. I was freezing and there was no way to get warm. My room was the last one, at the end of the hallway, on the north side of the building, and it was always very windy. My room had a big patio door and it wasn't well insulated. I could feel the cold air coming through and I was shivering. It was a long night but finally, François arrived in the morning to wake me up. He was surprised to find me there. He picked me up and put me in bed. It felt so good to be lying on something soft, and to be all wrapped up in my warm and cozy blankets. I asked François if he could leave me in bed for the morning, so I could get some sleep.

Shortly after my ordeal, Nellie informed me I would have to change rooms because there was a young woman moving in and there were no more rooms available. All the rooms that had an extra bed were occupied by male clients. I moved in with Henri to free up a room for her. It wasn't a big inconvenience for me because I liked Henri and he was easy to get along with. After my fall, I felt safer moving in with someone and Henri was glad to have me as his roommate. Things worked out just fine. We got along well. Henri was easy-going. He enjoyed my music and introduced me to some of his own music from his country: a place he was obviously proud of because he liked to talk about it all the time. He liked to reminisce about his friends and family there.

While I moved in his room, it was the time of the World Cup — the world's biggest soccer tournament. Henri's country was playing and everybody encouraged him by cheering for Chile. Henri told me that before he became ill, he played on his school's soccer team. He talked to me a lot about his past and the way things used to be; although, his life changed because of his illness, despite his debilitating disease, he still had a good sense of humor.

Nellie introduced me to the new girl who moved in to my room. Her name was Valerie. She moved around propelling herself with her feet, in a small, manual wheelchair. I could tell right away that she was intelligent and well-educated; however, she was somewhat apprehensive and uptight. She was polite with me, but I could sense she had no interest at all in meeting me.

She spent the first week in her room. She came out at night in the kitchen to have a snack before settling in for the night. I took advantage of that time to approach her and know her better. It took me a while but eventually we became friends. She wasn't the easiest person to get along with; she took life too seriously. She was a true feminist and gave me the impression she didn't like men at all. She was a well-educated woman who had a degree in criminology. I was careful with what I said because she didn't put up with anything that diminished women in any way. Things I thought were compliments, she took as an insult. I was often annoyed with her attitude and I let her know it. This would lead to a big argument and one of us ended up leaving, although, I truly believed sometimes, deep inside, we enjoyed those heated moments.

One day, Pascal came and asked if I could help him write a letter to a girl he had seen in a newspaper advertisement. I told him I was glad to. We agreed that he would come to the computer lab to see me after supper, when everything was quiet, so we had more privacy. He was funny! The first couple of letters we wrote were lies. He described himself as a tall, dark, muscular man in his twenties studying to become an open-heart surgeon. He made me laugh. I started to call him Arnold after Arnold Schwarzenegger; from then on, everybody at the center called him Arnold. I don't know if he felt guilty, but after a while, he told me he didn't feel comfortable lying to his correspondent and wanted to tell her the truth. When he revealed his true self, she took it well. She said she admired him and was glad he had disclosed his true identity. After doing so, Pascal lost all interest in writing to her. He stopped coming to visit me at the computer lab. I believed he was feeling sorry about his condition and the restraints it imposed on him.

One day after lunch, I went to my room to listen to music. My stereo system was mounted on a shelf on the wall, so I could press the buttons with my lips to operate the system. I couldn't see but I knew where everything was. I could operate everything without too much difficulty. I went in my room as usual, and I drove up to the shelving where my sound system was located and went to press the power button, but I was having trouble finding it. I thought it was a little unusual because I didn't normally have such difficulty. I tried a few times, but I couldn't find anything and that's when I finally realized that my stereo system was gone. I checked around to see if my speakers were still in their place but unfortunately they had also disappeared. What an awful feeling, like I was violated. The thought of someone coming into my private space and taking something away from me was such a shock. After regaining my composure, I went to get some help. As I was leaving my room, Nellie was coming down the hallway. I told her what happened and she quickly went to take a look. She confirmed what I told her and called security.

The guard did a security sweep and didn't find anything unusual. I could kiss my stereo goodbye. I, nevertheless, called the police to report my stolen goods because I needed a police report to file an insurance claim to recoup my losses.

Soon after I placed the call, I received a visit from two lovely female constables. They asked me a few questions, took some notes, and went on their way; they said they would do their best to retrieve my merchandise but the odds were slim.

Our latest arrival was a man in his mid-forties. It didn't take us long to know him. Robert was an unusual character. He looked like someone who appeared straight out of the nineteen fifties. He brushed his hair back in a duck-tail, and he wore a black leather jacket, T-shirt, and skin tight black leather pants, with black high heeled shoes. He was quite the picture. He sat in a raggedy, old wheelchair that was falling apart. He had no foot pedals and no cushion to sit comfortably. He stayed frozen in time. He was a nice person but had no social skills. He didn't know how to act around people. He was stubborn and didn't like anyone telling him what to do. He thought he was God's gift to women but he often clashed with them.

He came to the rehab to see if he could manage to live independently. He needed the help of several people to achieve his goal; he was so proud and obstinate, people had a hard time getting him to cooperate. In his mind, he had to prove to them he didn't need help from anyone. He didn't consider everything it took to move out on his own. He had to be pushed to do everything. He tried to pick up every girl he saw, but he was so awkward in his approach he didn't have much success. I was embarrassed at the lines he came out with. The funniest part was when he tried to pick up Valerie because she simply didn't give him a chance. She shot him down every time. I enjoyed seeing her set him straight. It was hilarious. But, putting aside his funny ways, Robert was a nice guy. He was helpful and extremely neat. Whenever he saw that one of us needed something, he always offered his assistance.

We often got together during the weekend to order food. Robert assisted those who needed help, in getting set up to eat. He was the most independent guy on the floor. He didn't need anyone's assistance. He could take care of himself. His illness just slowed him down, and took away some of his strength, coordination, hearing, and a little bit of his balance. When people spoke to him, he pretended he understood what they said but it was obvious by his reply that he didn't hear a thing.

Chapter 9

The boys and I decided we would go out and have some fun. Marc said he knew a good place to go. It was a popular strip club downtown. It wasn't something I would have chosen because of my visual impairment but I decided I would go anyway. I thought that it would be great to see how everybody would react around all those beautiful, naked women. I must admit I was frustrated at the thought of having all those females in their birthday suits dancing all around me. Nevertheless, everybody liked the idea, so we agreed to go the following Friday evening.

I had a major concern about going out with the boys; I was worried about what would happen if I had to use the washroom. It was a big problem because I needed help. I decided I would swallow my pride and wear a condom-catheter just like the ones the quadriplegics were using. I told Nellie about my idea and she thought it was great. She told me she would help me get the supplies and put it on for me Friday afternoon before she left for the weekend. I wasn't at ease with the idea but it was something I needed to do.

Friday arrived and Nellie came to see me in the living room to ask if I still wanted her to help me. I felt embarrassed at the thought of her putting a condom-catheter on me, but it was necessary if I wanted to go out with the boys and not worry about having to go to the toilet.

I thought of Nellie like a big sister. We had a good relationship. I liked her a lot and she was a good friend, but still I felt shy and nervous, and didn't know what to make of it all. I felt humiliated. Nellie noticed my embarrassment and told me not to worry; it was part of her job. She quickly slipped on the condom-catheter. It felt strange to have such a contraption. I didn't really trust it. I was hoping I could test it before we went out. I still had a few hours and I drank a lot in hope I could go before we left.

It was time to leave. Our bus arrived but unfortunately, I still didn't feel the urge to go. I was having a lot of trouble with my bladder at the time, so I didn't want to take a chance without some type of backup system.

We had a short bus ride over to the nightclub. When we arrived, I told Marc to take it slow, so I could find my way. We were used to this routine because I depended on him when we went out. I felt comfortable and safe with Marc because he was aware of my limitations. I always trusted Marc. He had good judgment.

Once we were out of the bus, we decided Marc would take the lead, I would follow close behind, and the rest would follow me. Once inside, I felt a little nervous because it was dark and the music was loud. There were bright lights flashing all around that blinded me. It was, for me, a very hostile environment. I could barely see Marc in front of me and I couldn't rely on my hearing to orient myself, but somehow we managed to make it to a table near the stage where the women were dancing.

It was hard for us to communicate because the music was too loud. One of the dancers came over to our table and asked if we wanted anything to drink. She smelled good and I only wished that I could see her. I asked her for a beer, and so did Marc and Henri, but Pascal and Robert ordered a screwdriver.

The boys were having a great time; from what they were telling me, the dancers were all beautiful. Needless to say, I wasn't enjoying myself as much as they were. I felt out of place but I have to admit, I had a few laughs anyway from listening to the guys with their silly remarks. After their first drink, the boys were already starting to feel the effects of the alcohol. Henri was particularly enjoying the scenery. His Latin blood was racing. He was funny and a real animal!

Pascal got one of the girls to come and dance at our table by giving her five dollars, and the boys really got a kick out of that. Robert enjoyed it so much that he got a different girl to come every once in a while. He must have gotten at least ten girls to come and strip at our table. I felt kind of stupid and out of place because I didn't know where to look or what I was looking at; I got some relief from drinking. The beer tasted good. After a couple of beers, I finally felt the urge to urinate but I held it in as long as I could because I didn't trust my condom-catheter to keep me dry. The time came when I couldn't hold it any longer. I let go and hoped that everything worked out.

I could feel the warmth of the urine flowing down into the tube, attached to my thigh, and going into the bag tied below my knee. Everything worked out marvelously. Shortly after, Marc let us know that he needed to go to the washroom, but we soon found out that the toilets were located in the basement and that they weren't wheelchair accessible. I was happy I decided to wear the condom-catheter because it made it so much easier. I didn't tell my friends about it because I was too proud. There was two hours to go before our pick-up. The fellows couldn't wait so long. They went outside to find a discrete area to relieve themselves. It wasn't as big of an inconvenience for Robert as it was for Marc because he needed someone to help him. Robert offered to literally give him a hand. They both felt uncomfortable but they didn't have a choice. Upon their return, they shared a few funny anecdotes about their little adventure.

I decided there and then, that was the last time I'd go to a strip joint. By the time our bus arrived to pick us up, I was smashed and my leg bag was full, so it was time to go. I was hoping I made it back before I had an overflow. Our bus finally arrived and we were on our way. Upon our arrival, Henri got the attendant to take him to the toilet. We could all hear him let out a big sigh of relief from the kitchen.

Chapter 10

One evening, while sitting alone in the kitchen, Valerie popped into my mind. I decided to visit her to see how she was doing. I went to her room but her door was shut. I stayed there for a minute or two, hesitating, wondering if I should knock or not when suddenly I heard her voice saying, "Randy, is that you? Come on in."

I let myself in, and Valerie was sitting in bed with her back against the wall, reading a book. So, I said to her, "Hello there, stranger. How have you been? I haven't seen you for a long time."

She replied, "I haven't been out of my room lately. I spend most of my time here reading because I don't feel like seeing anyone. I go to my therapies and I return here to read. I also speak with my friends on the telephone but that's about it." She said to me, "I am glad you came by because I was thinking of you a lot lately. I think we should have sex."

There were a lot of questions going through my mind. I felt intimidated never having slept with an intelligent, mature, and outspoken woman like Valerie, and I had conflicting thoughts about the entire matter. In a certain way, I felt excited about what was about to happen. On the other hand, I didn't feel secure because she was four years older than I. I figured she must have had much more experience than I but I tried to encourage myself by saying, "Stop beating yourself up. Relax and take it like it comes and everything will be all right."

The attendant came over as usual around ten thirty to put me in bed. He undressed me and gave me a quick wash. He made sure I was in a comfortable position for the night, covered me with a warm blanket, and left. There was nothing unusual about it; it was my normal bedtime routine.

Shortly after his departure, Valerie entered my room and positioned her wheelchair close to my bed and stood. She sat on the edge of the bed and pulled her nightgown over her head. She was completely naked. I caught a glimpse of her long, dark hair hanging down her back because it made quite a contrast on her milky white skin. After doing so, she lifted the blankets and snuggled close to me.

Valerie was afflicted with a rare form of arthritis that made her joints really stiff. She had very little flexibility. She was the complete opposite of me. There we were, both on our back lying next to each other. I wasn't sure how to approach her, when suddenly, she said to me, "What are you waiting for? Kiss me." I awkwardly turned on my side and kissed her. After doing so, she told me, "Make love to me."

I tried to get on top of her but I couldn't. I was completely exhausted, so she said, "Let me try." She managed to hoist herself on top of me, but once there she couldn't position herself well enough for us to connect. She was much too stiff. She returned on her back, visibly disappointed; we continued to caress and please each other within the limits of our physical conditions.

After we were through, we lay there quietly. I didn't feel good about myself, knowing I couldn't please her as much as she would have liked, but suddenly, she started to laugh and I asked her what was so funny. She told me, "Us, don't you think?" We both started to laugh. She stayed for the remainder of the night, and got up and left before the staff arrived for the day.

I didn't see Valerie until a few days later. She was coming down the hallway on her way to take her shower. I said hi to her but she didn't give me any response. She completely ignored me. My fear about our sexual encounter jeopardizing our friendship was well-founded. My theory was she realized that night how limited she was by her physical condition and her attitude made me feel uncomfortable. I felt I was less than a man because I couldn't satisfy her and she probably felt the same. I don't believe she understood until then how disabled she was.

Chapter 11

I was having a tremendously difficult time emptying my bladder and I had a sharp and throbbing pain in my lower back. I went over to the rehab clinic to see the doctor about it. I suspected it was a kidney infection as I had suffered one a few years back and I was experiencing similar symptoms. The doctor didn't agree with my diagnosis. He thought it was a muscle pain and told me he would speak to my physiotherapist to treat the area.

The therapist treated me with cold compresses along with a laser treatment but it didn't do the trick. My pain kept on increasing, and it became unbearable and I started to have a fever. The doctor came by and prescribed antibiotics. She was confident that, with the medicine, I would be back to normal in no time. Unfortunately, she was wrong; I got worse that evening. My fever increased and I was burning up. Despite my high temperature, I was freezing. I couldn't stop shaking. Nellie got the doctor to come. Following her examination, she told Nellie to call an ambulance. The emergency department was crowded and I was left alone in a busy hallway on an uncomfortable stretcher. I was so cold and weak from the fever. I felt scared and alone. I didn't know what was happening to me. A nurse came by to check my vital signs and asked a few questions about my condition.

Soon after, a doctor came to see me, examined me, gave a few orders to the nurse who was with him, and left without addressing a word to me. The next thing I knew, the nurse came over to insert a catheter. It was an unpleasant feeling and I didn't like it being done in the hallway in front of everyone, but I was simply too weak to complain. I just wanted them to make me better. After I was there for a long time, I was so thirsty but there was no one around who would give me a drink. I spent that night in the hallway without being able to get anyone to help me. I was miserable and needed to be repositioned. It was a very cold environment. I was weak, tired, scared, and I just wanted to get out of there. I wanted to go home to see a familiar face. I spent the rest of that night in the hallway with people going back and forth, ignoring my requests for water or to be repositioned. It was hard. I didn't want to spend another night like the one I just endured.

Nellie contacted my parents and told them of my predicament. They came over to see me later that morning. When they arrived, I was happy to see them and I wanted them to get me out of there; I didn't like the attitude of the staff or the way they neglected me. My parents asked to speak with the doctor about my condition to see if he could get me into a room where I could receive proper care. If not, they would take me back home to our local hospital where they could be close by and see that I got better attention.

The doctor didn't want me to go. He told my parents and me that it was a bad kidney infection, and he didn't want me to leave. He said they were perfectly capable of treating me there. I told him I didn't want to spend any more time in the hallway; I needed to be taken to a room. It was horrible; there were all kinds of people coming in and out of the emergency room area. There were people on drugs freaking out and a person that appeared to be schizophrenic. There were all kinds of scenarios. It was a real zoo!

The doctor promised he would do his best to get me a room on a unit as soon as possible. I finally got a room on the floor later that evening. I was relieved to be in a quieter place. I was put in a room with four beds and I was surprised upon my arrival that the room was occupied by three women. It was unusual; I wasn't used to sharing a hospital room with female roommates. I spent the next ten days there, and I had many roommates of both genders come and go.

They managed to treat my infection, but they didn't take the time to wash me or help me to go to the bathroom or reposition me. When it came to feeding me, they gave me blended food as fast as they could. There was no empathy or respect. I felt like an animal in the barn. Luckily, someone came from the rehab almost every day to wash me and make sure my basic needs were met.

My treatment was finally over and I left the hospital. I was glad to get out of there and I never wanted to go back. Unfortunately, before I left, the nurse gave me an appointment to see the urologist the following month.

Chapter 12

Back at rehab, I quickly resumed my regular schedule. I was happy to work at the computer again and to see my friends. I had a lot more energy.

We were in March and things were getting boring. One night, while we were all in the kitchen talking about how we couldn't wait for summer to arrive, all of a sudden Robert said, "Why don't we have a party?" Everybody agreed that a party was a good idea. Valerie was sitting at the table silently eating a bowl of cereal, when she said, "If you want to make a party, you have to get organized. You have to decide what kind of party you want and who would be responsible for planning it."

Valerie's intervention brought on a serious conversation. We met with the coordinator and she was willing to help us. She said, "Let me lay down the ground rules. You will have my complete support. I would like to have a weekly detailed report. If I am satisfied with your efforts, I will give you permission to have your party. And to help you start, I will give you a budget of three-hundred dollars to cover expenses." So far, so good; we got together that evening to make a plan. We met in the kitchen after supper and Valerie wrote down all that was said. We decided it would be a beach party to take away the winter blues. We established that everyone who took part in our committee would take on some sort of responsibility; we discussed what was needed to make the party a success. We agreed to have good music, entertainment, food, drinks, and decorations.

Robert and Marc chose to take care of the music. Pascal took on the decorations, and I was left to provide the food and drinks. Valerie was in charge of writing the reports and making sure everyone did their part.

Our party project was a good idea. It took away the monotony of our everyday routines; we didn't worry about our aches and pains. Things were moving along and everyone did a good job. Marc and Robert arranged to get a sound system and recorded the music appropriate for the evening. Robert was the disc jockey. Pascal rented a couple of palm trees and a few inflatable swimming pools, posters to put on the walls, beach balls and a few other little trinkets. I got a major brewery to donate the beer and they gave us some coolers that were appropriate for the occasion. I obtained from our local Coca-Cola Company all the pop that we needed, and as for the food, I was lucky enough to get the help of a major sponsor who was happy to answer my request.

We continued our weekly meetings with the coordinator of the rehab center. She was impressed with the way everything was organized; therefore, she gave us permission to go ahead with our project.

One month before the party, we needed to get some publicity out and fast. Valerie and I printed a bunch of flyers to be distributed by the rehab center, which was the core of a big organization that branched out to different areas of the city. It was affiliated with a few group homes and a number of apartments that had twenty-four hour care. They also served a large number in the community with their daily rehab clinic. We estimated we'd get around one-hundred people.

The arts and crafts department made posters to put up. Things were looking good. I got a large number of volunteers to help us with attendant care and serve drinks. We hoped everything would be okay, although I wasn't one-hundred per cent sure about Robert being our disc jockey because he could be outrageous and irresponsible at times. I hoped for the best. We asked people coming to the party to dress in beach wear but it wasn't a requirement. Everyone would certainly be welcomed. It was going to be a great party. Pascal had T-shirts made for our group of organizers with the letters BEACH PARTY MAN on them and they were cool.

During that time, I had to go back to the hospital. Annie volunteered to come with me. I felt somewhat apprehensive going back, especially since I didn't know what was in store. It was an examination of my bladder. The nurse technician was waiting for me. She seemed relieved to see me arrive. In the examination room, Annie helped me put on a blue gown. It was the first time she saw me undressed. I was shy. She then helped me to the washroom to get a urine sample. Annie and the nurse got me on the examining table in another compromising position. The nurse used an electronic probe to measure the contractions of my bladder. It was a painful procedure. The nurse invited us to sit at her desk. The questions she asked took me by surprise. Questions like, was I continent, able to have an erection, sexually active? Annie was there listening and I felt totally uncomfortable! Before leaving, she told me she would send the results of my exam to the doctor.

Our beach party was the next day. Our group met that evening to make sure we didn't forget anything. The following morning, I got up earlier than usual to go downstairs to wait for the beer delivery. Volunteers filled the refrigerators with drinks and stored the munchies. Pascal couldn't decorate until breakfast and lunch were over. Robert and Marc prepared everything for the musical entertainment. It was time. Things were looking good. Many people came from the community. Even the quads came to give us support. Everybody was having fun. We had a large group of volunteers, attendants, and staff; even though they didn't have to work, they came of their own free will. The staff at rehab made us feel like we were part of a big family. I felt lucky to be there.

I was happy to see that Virgil and Sandra showed up. Virgil congratulated me on the party. I was proud to get such a positive reaction from him; I was happy to know he appreciated my efforts. I knew I didn't do it on my own, and that the others also needed the recognition for a job well done, but I appreciated the acknowledgments.

Pascal did great with the decorations. He was quite amazing. He put two giant inflatable palm trees with two little swimming pools filled with beach sand; inside there were toys to play with, along with many other small decorations here and there.

Marc and Robert also did a great job with the music. I was relieved and surprised with the way Robert handled everything despite his occasional crazy comments on the PA system.

Valerie came to check it out but only for a little while. She didn't stay long but she was pleasantly satisfied with the outcome. The party lasted until one a.m. but the majority of people left before eleven. Most of the people who stayed were the gang from my unit. We ended up going to bed around three thirty in the morning.

Chapter 13

Now that the party was over, things were back to normal. I worked from Monday to Friday at the computer, and sometimes during the evening, to find better ways to run my software. It was all interesting but I needed some other kind of distraction — something to help me relax. I decided to try swimming again. I went over to the volunteer office to see if I could get someone to accompany me.

Upon my arrival, I asked if I could speak to Brian. He was in charge of the volunteers for the rehab. He was a nice man. He was well-dressed and had an engaging smile. He liked to joke around. He was one of the people who helped make our party a success. He was easy-going and he enjoyed his work.

I asked Brian if he could find somebody to take me swimming. He said he would contact me so we could get acquainted beforehand. The following Monday, Brian called to inform me he found someone. He was a huge man. At first, I was uncomfortable by his presence. I never saw such a large man. He must have weighed four-hundred pounds or more. I felt like a pretzel beside him. My first reaction was that I didn't want him to take me swimming. He was strange; he didn't smile and looked angry. Then, I decided I was being prejudiced because of his extreme obesity. I would give him a chance.

We went swimming that day, even though I wasn't comfortable around him. I didn't know what to think. He was bizarre. I was nervous alone with him. He wasn't gentle. He practically ripped off my clothes; I decided there and then it was the last time. The swim went well and I was fortunate I didn't need his help inside the pool. I could maneuver on my own with the help of a little floating device. It felt great to be back in the water. After one hour in the pool, I was cold and dreading that Mr. Humongous would touch me again. It wasn't a pretty picture. I thought, how do you get yourself into these predicaments? He dropped me in my chair and dressed me. I felt like I had just gone three rounds with a Japanese sumo wrestler. My socks, pants, and sweater were on my body all twisted out of place. I was sitting in my wheelchair all crooked to the point where I had a lot of difficulty driving my chair.

Mr. Humongous followed me back to the rehab and we parted at the reception area. I thanked him for his help and I told him I would let him know if I needed his assistance again.

After he left, I hurried back up to my unit; I had an urgent need to void. Annie was sitting on the couch watching television and when she saw me, she called me over. When I got close, she said, "What happened to you? You look like you were in an accident."

I told her I was in a big fight with a sumo wrestler. She laughed and said, "What are you talking about?"

I said I would explain everything to her once I went to the bathroom. I really needed to go! I asked her if she knew where Richard was. She told me he was on the other side. She offered to help. What a relief. After my ordeal at the hospital, I no longer felt uncomfortable with Annie giving me personal care. Looking back at the whole situation, I truly believe it was a good thing it happened because it brought us much closer. She was a decent person and very respectable. I felt special having her as a friend. We shared a lot together; we had a mutual respect for each other. I could trust her with anything.

Chapter 14

One day I was sitting in the living room listening to music on the radio, when suddenly, I started hearing these strange sounds coming from the hallway. I went over to see what it was. Nellie introduced me to Michael, a small guy in a powered wheelchair with a funny appearance. He could not speak and he used a long pointer made out of what appeared to be a clothes hanger strapped on his forehead. His arms and legs were strapped to his chair because he was too spastic; he looked like some kind of prehistoric creature. When he laughed, he let out an unusual wailing sound. He was dangerous to be around but, considering all his disabilities, he managed fairly well. On both sides of his chair was a set of sound speakers. In the back where the batteries were, he connected a cassette deck. He could operate the system with a switch mounted on his communication board that was resting over his lap, on the arm rest of the chair. Before he left, he turned on a switch on his table with the pointer attached to his forehead. The music started playing. He took off with the music blasting out loud and wailing down the hallway. He was quite imposing; he couldn't go without being noticed.

Nellie told me that Michael came by looking for his friend Jean Luc, who was one of the attendants. I met Jean Luc for the first time that evening. He was working with us. I discovered upon meeting him that he was quite the character. He was a strong, muscular man, fairly tall with long hair and a bushy beard. He was a jovial man, who gave the impression he didn't have a care in the world. I learned later on that Jean Luc had a university degree in physics. He was very interesting. He and Michael were the best of friends. Whenever Jean Luc was working, Michael was around and followed him everywhere and often got in his way. Eventually, Jean Luc had to tell him not to come around so often when he was working. He was previously warned by the management to do his job because he was interrupting his work; despite his warnings, he occasionally showed up anyway.

    I became good friends with Michael. He couldn't speak and I couldn't see what he wanted to tell me, so the only way we could communicate was to have someone read what he was trying to say by pointing at certain letters or images on his communication board. He used the pointer mounted on his forehead to indicate whatever message he wanted to convey. The board had certain distinct and common images to facilitate everyday tasks; for example: if he wanted a drink, he had the image of someone having a drink. It was designed to speed up whatever he wanted to say.

    Michael had a girlfriend who was also severely disabled; she had cerebral palsy like him. She couldn't speak and she had uncontrollable movements in her arms, legs, and facial muscles. I didn't quite understand, at the time, the relationship they had but they seemed to like each other a lot despite their obvious constraints. One day, Michael came over to invite me out for supper at his favorite restaurant. Jean Luc was my interpreter. Michael said we would be going with Jean Luc and he invited his girlfriend. I gladly accepted his invitation. I reserved my bus for the following Friday.

    Jean Luc gave me the address of the restaurant. It was in downtown Montréal. I felt a little apprehensive at the idea of going downtown on my own, although Jean Luc reassured me he would be at the restaurant waiting. My bus arrived on time to pick me up in my manual chair. Jean Luc was waiting for me with Michael and Jessica. The restaurant wasn't wheelchair accessible. We went through a narrow alleyway that led us to a small back door with a little step. For Jessica and Michael, it was a problem with their powered chairs but, with the help of a restaurant employee, they managed.

So, there we were, inside a fancy Italian restaurant. It took Jean Luc and the waiter a while to get everyone seated properly. Jean Luc was a big clown. Michael and Jessica loved him. He made them laugh and wail out loud, and at the same time they moved their arms and legs with their uncontrollable muscle spasms. We attracted many onlookers. They were curious and somewhat perplexed. I'm sure they never expected such a scene before coming to the restaurant. What was to be a quiet, relaxing meal turned into something quite different; Jean Luc came prepared. He brought a backpack with everything he needed to complete his task. Once we were all settled in, a lovely young waitress came by to ask us if we would like anything to drink. Jean Luc was constantly making remarks about the people in the restaurant and the way they were looking at us. The more Jean Luc spoke, the more Michael burst out laughing, creating a loud ruckus, and causing Jessica to follow suit. I must say, I was impressed with the attitude of the restaurant employees. They were all helpful; they seemed to be getting a kick out of serving their unusual customers but I wasn't quite persuaded that all the customers were sharing the same sentiments.

Michael and Jessica ordered spaghetti, and Jean Luc and I shared a pizza. Jean Luc's hands were full feeding himself, Michael, and Jessica. I was sitting at the table with Jean Luc, who was standing across the table in front of me, with Jessica on his left and Michael on his right, who were both facing each other. Jean Luc draped them both with towels, so they didn't mess up their clothes. Due to their condition, whenever they ate or drank, they had to swallow their food and drinks in gulps because they couldn't really chew their food; therefore, the process of eating was often messy. Michael was drinking a lot and feeling no pain. He was having a great time. I was amazed at how much he could drink and what a good appetite he and Jessica had; even though they were both small, they could really pack it in. Jean Luc gave a mouthful of food to one and then the other, and at the same time he snuck in a bite for himself. Luckily, I could manage to eat on my own. He didn't have to worry about me. After a little while, things got messy. Michael was getting louder. He would burst out laughing, causing his food to go flying out of his mouth. There was food all over him and all around the area where we were. It was a real disaster zone.

Jessica, on the other hand, was well-behaved and not quite so messy. I sense that we were beginning to draw a little too much attention to our table and I felt self-conscious. It was time to go. I was no longer enjoying myself. Once our meal was over, Jean Luc put everything away and cleaned up Michael, Jessica, and the mess around us. We hurried because it was already time to go outside and wait for the bus to pick us up. A bus arrived as we were exiting; unfortunately, it wasn't mine. It was for Michael and Jessica. Jean Luc helped to get them onto the bus and sent them both on their way. Jean Luc asked me if I would be all right while I was waiting for my bus to arrive. I told him I was fine and he didn't need to worry about me. He left on his bicycle and I was feeling a little nervous waiting in the middle of downtown Montréal. I couldn't really see, but I could hear footsteps and parts of conversations, smell perfume and other different types of odors: some more pleasant than others.

Something embarrassing happened while I was waiting. A woman approached me, putting some spare change in my hands, saying, "God bless you and have a nice day." Everything happened so unexpectedly, and before I could say anything, she was gone. I wanted to tell her, "No, thank you! I don't need your money; it's not what it appears to be. I'm just waiting for the bus," but it was too late. She was gone. I thought it was kind of funny and I couldn't wait to get back to rehab to tell Annie about it.

Chapter 15

Shortly after that evening, Nellie came to inform me I would be moving next door to help balance the workload. I didn't see a problem since Nellie would still be my educator and I would just be across the corridor from my friends.

I moved the following Monday and my new roommate arrived: an unfriendly man in his late fifties with a big chip on his shoulder. He was a real cold fish. I made a big mistake accepting to cross over to the other side — my roommate snored like a grizzly bear. I had never heard anything like it. I couldn't sleep and was consequently exhausted. I couldn't focus either. It affected my appetite, too. What a nightmare. It went on like that for a month until I became ill. My kidneys were bothering me again. This time, I had no pain, although, I came down with a very high fever and I was going into shock. Nellie called the doctor; he examined me, checked my vital signs, and sent me to the hospital right away.

François, my attendant, accompanied me in the ambulance. Once at the hospital, I was examined right away and transferred to a different area to a small room with eight beds. There wasn't much room for the nursing staff to get around and no room for privacy.

Once I was settled in, a nurse came to install an intravenous line. I was so weak, I could hardly move a muscle; but luckily, François stayed with me until his shift was over. Before he left, he made sure I was okay and reassured me someone would come by to see me the next day. He gave me a kiss; my initial reaction was one of surprise and confusion but, shortly after, I felt a warm feeling because I felt I was with someone who cared. I didn't feel safe. I couldn't move a muscle; I didn't have a call bell if I needed help. Finally, later that evening, I was transferred to the second floor to a room with two beds. It was much nicer and quieter. A nurse came shortly after my arrival to check my vital signs, and my intravenous, and set me up with a call bell that I could operate easily by pressing a flat circular pad with my elbow.

My first night there was hard because I couldn't sleep, even though I was weak and tired. I was always ringing the call bell to get a nurse to come and give me the urinal; but after a few times, the nurse finally left the urinal between my legs. If I needed to void I could just try to and I didn't have to worry about wetting myself. The nurse who took care of me that night was a cold fish who didn't smile or show any sign of compassion. I had a long and unpleasant night.

The following morning wasn't any better. The nurse who came by to give me breakfast put the food tray in front of me and started to leave. I had to let her know I needed help. She turned around and asked what I wanted. I told her I needed to be fed. She told me she didn't have time right away and she would return to feed me later on because she had too many things to do. She returned about an hour later and my food was cold. She began feeding me by stuffing the food down my throat as fast as she could. I told her to slow down, and did momentarily, but then started again. I gave up. I told her I wasn't hungry because my food was cold and her attitude made me lose my appetite.

The doctor came by later on that morning to tell me I had a severe kidney infection but I shouldn't worry because they had it under control. The antibiotics were doing the trick. The bad news was I had to remain in the hospital for ten days until I completed my treatment. I was disappointed at the thought of having to stay but I was happy they could fix my problem.

Nellie dropped in to see me that afternoon. She told me that she was glad I was on the mend but I gave them quite a scare. She asked how the care was. I said it wasn't very good and hygiene wasn't on top of their priority list as they hadn't washed me since my arrival. I took the opportunity to ask if she could remove the urinal between my legs. I told her it was a constant problem every time I needed to get the urinal emptied. She suggested that I try to wear a condom-catheter because it would probably make things a lot easier. When the nurse returned, we talked to her about it and she said it was probably a good idea, but she would have to verify if they had any condom-catheters on the unit.

Nellie stayed a while longer. Before leaving, she helped position me in bed and made sure I wasn't in need of anything. On her way out, she stopped to talk to the nurse manager to see if I could see an occupational therapist and if she could get me a better mattress. The one I had was uncomfortable. I needed something softer to prevent pressure sores. A nurse came over shortly after Nellie left, with a condom-catheter and told me she had never installed one. She was a young girl who wasn't much more than twenty years old. Considering her age and her lack of experience, I didn't feel secure. She tried her best. It took her a while to get it on but something about it didn't seem right. I asked if she could fix it but she told me it was okay the way it was. I wasn't at all persuaded but I didn't insist. I suspected that she felt a little embarrassed. Shortly after she left, it was time to see if everything was functioning. I began to void, fearing I would wet myself, but everything worked fine. There didn't seem to be leakage; maybe I was wrong but I was still doubtful.

I was still having a difficult time emptying my bladder. It was impossible for me to get any rest, even though I had the condom-catheter. I finally managed to fall asleep, only to wake up wet shortly after. The condom-catheter had sprung a leak; I rang the call bell for someone to come and change my sheets, and the two nurses who arrived were surprisingly friendly. They put clean sheets on the bed and removed the condom-catheter because it wasn't serving its purpose; before they left, they positioned the urinal snugly between my legs to avoid any further accidents. I spent most of the night awake because my bladder was really uncomfortable. That morning before breakfast, another doctor came to see me. He told me he would schedule a bladder examination as soon as possible.

The morning went by slowly. I was expecting someone to come by to give me a wash but nobody came. The next thing I knew, it was lunchtime. An orderly came to feed me. I was presented with pureed food and he stuffed it in my mouth as fast as he could. After my main course was over, he asked me if I would like to have some soup. Before I knew it, he stuck a large syringe into my mouth, pressing down on the plunger and injecting the food down my throat; as soon as I realized what he did, I got angry and told him to go away. I was totally disgusted by his attitude. He had no respect and he made me feel like an animal. I was upset and not at all impressed with the care given to me in that hospital.

The remainder of the day was boring. Just when I thought no one would come, Nellie showed up. I was extremely happy to see her. I told her about the poor care I was receiving and she told me she would get somebody to come by the next day. I was relieved to hear that. She stayed to help me with my supper. Before leaving, she made sure I was comfortable. I had another long, strenuous night and I couldn't sleep. I constantly had the urge to void and it prevented my rest.

The following morning after breakfast, a porter took me to a brightly lit room and it was freezing. They transferred me onto the examining table and put my legs up in stirrups. What an embarrassing position. A nurse disinfected my genital area with a cold substance. The doctor informed me he would be injecting something into my urethra to minimize the pain. After doing so, he inserted a catheter. It was equipped with a camera. He said everything looked normal; I just seemed to have a lazy bladder.

Back in my room, I was hoping someone from rehab was there but unfortunately, it didn't happen. I felt disappointed and lonely; I wanted to see a friendly face. I was tired of having to deal with uptight, stressed out people at the hospital. I was feeling dirty and I needed to go to the washroom. I hadn't had a bowel movement in six days. I didn't trust the nurses so I was waiting for an attendant from rehab to come and help me, but the afternoon went by and no one came. I was discouraged.

A nurse came by after supper and told me Nellie called to say she was sorry that no one came to see me but someone would come the next day for sure. It was reassuring to know I wasn't forgotten. Later that evening, I was so uncomfortable, I knew I had to do something or I wouldn't be able to sleep. I rang the call bell to get help to the washroom. A young, visibly stressed nurse came; she told me she would see what she could do and left. I waited a long time but she didn't return, so I rang the call bell again. A different nurse showed up; I told her I would need a suppository. Once she was done, she slipped a diaper on me. I felt angry and embarrassed to be put in such an undignified position and I told her so, but I lost that argument. I had to resign myself. It wasn't a pleasant feeling to have to soil myself; I felt disgusted and powerless. After I was done, I rung for someone to clean me up. Finally, after approximately one hour, two nurses came. I wanted to get back to rehab where people really cared. I was tired of being in bed and tired of feeling dirty. I just wanted to go back to rehab, where I could take a shower, sit on the toilet, eat good food, and be treated with dignity and respect.

The following morning after breakfast, I got a pleasant surprise. François arrived with my power wheelchair. I was happy to see him. It was so nice to see a familiar face. He took a good look at me and said, "You look like you could use a bath." He gathered all the necessary supplies, and took me to the bathroom and then to the bathtub. It felt so good to submerge myself into all that warmth. François dressed me and sat me in my wheelchair. It felt really good to be mobile again; François stayed to have lunch with me but, unfortunately, he had to leave shortly after.

I felt like I was a whole new person — clean and comfortable. It was funny: now that I was up and mobile, I couldn't wait to get out of the place. It was noisy, dirty, and crowded and I really missed rehab and its people.

The next day, I received a visit from Annie. I was happy to see her. She told me that her friend, Robert, was working at the hospital as an intern in the field of neuro-ophthalmology and he was coming to visit us shortly.

Soon after, Robert arrived with a colleague. They both stayed a little while and chatted. Before leaving, Robert gave Annie a kiss on the lips; that's when I realized that Robert was more than a friend. I found it strange that in all the time we spent together, she never told me she was seeing someone. Throughout all our conversations, Robert never came up. Before leaving, Annie made sure I was all right and not in need of anything in particular, gave me a kiss on both cheeks, and went on her way.

The following day, the doctor came by to tell me that everything was okay with me and I could be discharged. I was happy, and I couldn't wait to get back to rehab to resume my work with the computer and see my friends.

Chapter 16

Nellie came shortly after to pick me up. I was truly glad to see her and to get out of that miserable place. Upon my return at the rehab, I resumed my daily routines. It was great to be back. I had much more energy to burn than before. I felt like a whole new person. What certainly helped a lot was that I changed rooms. I was no longer with that human chainsaw, who kept me up all night with his snoring. I moved in with Patrick, a young man in his late twenties who had become a quadriplegic after a car crash. I liked Patrick; he was a cool guy. We had similar interests. We were both ambitious; even though we had many physical barriers.

Patrick worked hard every day to overcome his disabilities. He had a very good attitude and I found him to be courageous. He had an engaging personality. I liked him a lot. I found it to be a very rewarding experience sharing a room with Patrick. I could see a lot of myself in him, in the way that he tried to overcome every obstacle that prevented him from being as independent as possible. He got frustrated and angry at times, but he never gave up and that is what I admired the most about him.

Patrick was great friends with another quad named Alfred. They did everything together and they encouraged each other by competing against one another; although, they also gave each other tricks to gain more of their independence. Patrick had a major advantage over Alfred because his injury wasn't quite as severe as his friend's. He had a little more movement and things were a lot easier for him to do, but Alfred was stubborn, persistent, and proud. He always tried to keep up with his buddy, even though it took him twice as much effort to get anything done. Alfred was a shy and reserved person, and he didn't mingle too much with the other residents. He only liked to hang around with Patrick.

Patrick had another major advantage over Alfred because he became a quadriplegic due to an automobile accident; therefore, he was fully compensated by the Québec automobile insurance plan. They paid for all the equipment he needed to facilitate his rehabilitation. His wheelchair was a super high-tech, light-weight vehicle and he had a special handicapped accessible automobile with all the latest gadgets to make it possible for him to operate. His insurance also paid to make his home wheelchair accessible and for basically everything else that he needed to function in life. Unfortunately, Alfred wasn't so lucky simply because his accident didn't happen on the road. He was swimming at his brother's house, and took a dive into the pool and broke his neck. So, he had no insurance coverage and because of that, he depended on the welfare system and it was nothing compared to what Patrick could obtain. It was a constant battle for him to get any type of equipment that he needed to become less dependent.

I couldn't help but think that the situation was unfair. They both had similar disabilities with similar needs, but simply because one person was lucky enough to be covered by insurance, he got everything he required to regain his autonomy. But the other person, who had no insurance, had to struggle to get the strict necessities to survive. To me, it wasn't right.

Chapter 17

The winter was finally over, and everybody welcomed the arrival of spring. With the warm weather quickly approaching, people enjoyed every moment after spending most of the winter indoors. It was amazing how the weather changed everyone; everybody got a burst of energy. People were smiling and enjoying the weather, and when they had a moment of free time, they went out soaking in the sun. Most of the people were outside on their balconies and the second floor patio. There were people circulating freely up and down the streets and sidewalks with their wheelchairs. All the windows from every building were open to let in the fresh air. It was amazing how a change of season made a difference.

I took the opportunity to go out and explore a little of the environment around rehab. I enjoyed the challenge of going out on my own. I first began by going across the street to where I went to exercise and swim every now and then. Slowly and gradually, I expanded my horizons. I took it upon myself to go farther and farther away from the rehab center. It was scary but I liked the challenge, and I knew my limits and remained vigilant. The area around the rehab was quiet. There wasn't much traffic around; therefore, I could rely on my hearing to help me move safely.

I started to follow Patrick and Alfred down the street to a little park. It was a quiet place that allowed us to get away from rehab.

The weather kept on improving and we took advantage of every free moment to go outside and enjoy the warm temperatures.

I went shopping down the street with Marc or to get some food to bring back to rehab to eat with our friends. Marc drove a scooter and he was a cautious fellow; I trusted him fully. I had to because I completely depended on his better judgment to get us to our destination safely. I followed right behind him. He had a bright red backpack mounted on the rear of his scooter. Through my eyes, it looked like a red, blurry spot. I stayed close and tried to keep my eyes on it to orient myself. Marc was good. He was aware of my dependence on him to circulate safely; even though we both took many risks, we were nevertheless careful.

It was freaky and scary for me whenever we crossed a major roadway. My adrenaline started to flow. It was weird. Many times I found myself praying to God I would make it across in one piece. My major problem going where the traffic was busy was the noise it created because I couldn't rely on my sense of hearing. All I could depend on was that blurry, red spot. I remember going down the sidewalks on a busy street with people all over, going up and down and not really paying attention to where they were going. If only they knew who they were dealing with, they would be more careful.

I had a good time that summer. Things were quiet at rehab since most of the employees were on vacation. There wasn't too much going on. I met a new girl who worked there as a volunteer. One day, I was sitting outside in the shade, enjoying the cool breeze, when she came and sat on the bench beside me and introduced herself and asked me my name. She told me she was working in the arts and crafts department, and asked if I would be interested in doing any type of arts and crafts. I told her I wasn't really keen on this it. With my poor vision and lack of mobility, I couldn't do much on my own.

She seemed to be a nice girl. She stayed talking with me a while. Before she left, she invited me to go to her department. She told me that even though I wasn't interested in doing any arts and crafts, I was welcome to stop by and say hello.

The following day, it was raining, windy, and cold. I couldn't really go outside and there wasn't much to do inside. The morning was quiet, so I decided to stay in my room and listen to music, but after a while it got to be boring. Suddenly, I thought of Mary Jane and decided to go down and see her in the arts and crafts department.

We became friends. She was an artist and mingled with all kinds of artists. We went out many times that summer and she introduced me to her circle of friends: painters, musicians, actors, producers, etc. I discovered that Mary Jane was an actress who played in a popular television series on one of the French stations. She also hosted a radio program on a local station. One particular night, she invited me downtown to see her perform. She was singing in a small nightclub. It was a great atmosphere. I sat at a table with her friends. Many of them were famous people who were mostly writers, performers, and musicians. She had a good voice but I didn't really like her repertoire, it wasn't really my style of music.

She invited me to go see a group who were performing in a very popular nightclub in downtown Montréal. Shortly after we were there, two of her friends arrived and sat with us; Mary Jane introduced them to me, and much to my surprise, I happened to be in the presence of two famous singers. They were both popular at the time. Their music was constantly playing on the French radio stations and they were being interviewed regularly on television and performing. They were also known to be beautiful women. One of them was portrayed as a famous sex symbol in Québec. I was impressed and amazed that I was sitting with these three beautiful women, although I couldn't help but feel like I didn't belong there. Mary Jane never ceased to impress me; she knew all kinds of people and everybody seemed to like to be with her. I appreciated her friendship but there was something about being around those people that made me feel uneasy. They were all interesting but I didn't fit in.

After that night, I didn't see Mary Jane, but it was probably for the best because I didn't feel like I belonged in her circle of friends. We didn't have anything in common. It's too bad; I still liked her. She was a lovely girl and I was going to miss her. There were rumors going around that she had a major confrontation with the coordinator of the rehab center and was subsequently dismissed. I wasn't at all surprised to hear such talk because she previously disagreed with certain practices that went on at the center. She wasn't one to obey the rules and she was downright defiant at times. It wasn't her first altercation with the coordinator and I suppose she finally pushed things too far.

Chapter 18

We had a new attendant working with us that summer. His name was Peter. I used to hang around with him; during his lunch break we often went down to the park. We usually stopped at the corner store to get something to take with us to eat there. He was a nice fellow. I really liked him; he was cool and easy-going. During that period, there was a series of robberies at the rehab. Nellie warned me to be careful with my money.

Approximately a month after the first robbery, I began to suspect I was missing money in my wallet; but I wasn't quite sure because it was never a large quantity. One day I was on my way to the park with Peter and suddenly it hit me: I said to myself, I bet he's the one ripping everybody off. The reason I came to that conclusion is that I kept my wallet in my backpack mounted on the back rest of my wheelchair; it was always with me. It was virtually impossible for anyone to steal money from me without me noticing it. The only time someone could take money from me was whenever I asked somebody to take money out of my wallet to buy something. I thought about everybody that I let manipulate my money and I came to the conclusion that Peter was the person I trusted least. I frequently asked him to take money out of my wallet to buy me something at the corner store. He always told me how much he took and how much he brought back in change. I trusted him and I never thought he would steal from me. I guess I was too naïve but the more I thought about it, the more I was convinced he was the one taking money from the people at the rehab center and from me.

My newest revelation bothered me. Later that evening, I devised a plan but I needed an accomplice. I got the help of my buddy Robert to count my money and he told me I had twenty-seven dollars: one twenty dollars bill, one five dollar bill, and one two dollar bill. After verifying, I went in the living room and asked Peter if he could go downstairs to get me a drink. He agreed with no hesitation. He took my wallet out of my backpack, opened it up and told me I didn't have change and he would take a two dollar bill and bring back the change. After leaving to go downstairs, I quickly went to Robert to count my money again. He said I only had twenty dollars left, so I knew he took more than two dollars to buy my pop. When he came back, he took out my wallet to put away the remainder of the change, gave me my drink, and left. After he was gone, I went to see Robert once again to count my money. He checked my wallet and told me I only had twenty dollars and a bit of loose change. My suspicion was confirmed. I got Robert to call downstairs to the coordinator to ask her to come to see me in my room as soon as possible.

She arrived within minutes. She entered my room, discreetly closed the door behind her, and asked what was going on. I explained what happened. She was interested in my findings but she told me to be quiet about it; that she would deal with the problem on the following Monday. I promised her I wouldn't say a word to anyone before the matter was dealt with.

Shortly after the coordinator left, Peter entered my room and asked me suspiciously what the coordinator was doing in my room. Without hesitating, I told him that she came to ask me some advice on what to get Sandra for her birthday. I thought of that excuse because it was something that was on my mind. I didn't know what to get her and her birthday was coming up. Peter was obviously relieved by my response and didn't suspect we had him figured out.

Monday morning, Peter was called down to the coordinator's office and he was given an ultimatum. He would either have to confess and admit that he was the one who was stealing the money from the residents, or they would call the police and he would most likely have a criminal record, making it very difficult for him to obtain any kind of employment elsewhere. He had no other choice but to admit his wrong doing. Following his confession, he was immediately fired.

Chapter 19

One Friday afternoon in August, there wasn't much going on. I was the only one in my group who stayed there that weekend; Richard, who was one of my attendants, suggested that we take advantage of the situation and go down to Montréal Road to do a bit of shopping. I said I would go if he didn't walk too fast in order for me to follow him. He was known to easily get distracted, but he promised he wouldn't walk so fast and he would look out for me. I felt a little reassured by his response but I wasn't quite convinced. Nevertheless, I took him up on his offer. It was better than staying at the rehab doing nothing.

Our outing went well until Richard had a moment of distraction; he wasn't paying attention to me. We were going down a busy sidewalk and there were people everywhere. They were all around and getting in between me and Richard; I lost sight of him at times but when I got to a clearing, I hurried to catch up with him. We were approaching a crosswalk and I was going as fast as I could, trying to keep up. He was distracted. When we arrived where we needed to get off the sidewalk to cross the street, instead of going down to the wheelchair slope Richard took a shortcut and went where there was no wheelchair access. I won't forget that day.

I was following right behind him; suddenly, I felt this jolt and I was propelled forward. I was almost thrown out of my chair. It happened so fast, it scared the daylights out of me! I lost control of my wheelchair and it was going toward oncoming traffic but I managed to regain control just in time to make it across the street.

Richard witnessed the entire scene. He felt guilty because he was distracted. He was very concerned about my well-being AND I reassured him I was okay. Still, he apologized several times to the point where I was getting annoyed. I told him to forget about it.

The rest of the summer was reasonably uneventful. I spent most of my days outdoors enjoying the beautiful weather. I went to work on the computer every now and then, so I wouldn't forget what I learned, although I knew everything I needed to be able to read and write using the computer. I was familiar with my programs and I no longer considered them much of a challenge, but I still enjoyed spending time at the computer. It was a great pastime for me.

Chapter 20

In September, Nellie introduced me to a young woman from France. Her name was Monique. She came to the rehab on an exchange project to learn how everything concerning rehabilitation facilities functioned in Canada. She had a warm approach and I liked her accent. Nellie informed me that Monique was staying with us for six months. I welcomed her and told her I was looking forward to working with her; later on, Nellie asked if I was willing to let her work with me. In her country she acted as an occupational therapist in a group home with children under sixteen, with mental and physical disabilities. The definition of an occupational therapist in France was different from what we knew. Her job consisted of taking care of every aspect of her clients' needs. She did everyday chores like cooking, cleaning, and laundry, taking care of their physical needs, and teaching them basic life skills.

I was awakened the very next day by Nellie and Monique. Nellie came to show her what she needed to do to get me started for the day. Nellie took care of me while Monique watched. My morning routine wasn't too complicated and things went fast. Monique seemed at ease with what she had to do. Once I was up, she followed me around throughout the day so that she could witness what was involved in my rehabilitation. It gave her the chance to meet all my therapists and other people I dealt with during the day.

She was impressed with what she saw, especially with the way they adapted the computer to satisfy my needs and how I could operate it. She caught on to my routine right away. I enjoyed her care. She was gentle, attentive, with a great sense of humor. During the next few weeks, she continued to accompany me to all my appointments, but after, she only came occasionally to enable Nellie to show her other aspects of the functioning of the center. It was pleasant to have her around. It was a rewarding experience.

Chapter 21

With summer ending, everybody was back at work. The rehab center was busy. There was a constant movement throughout the building. During the day, there was no time to be bored but the evening was a different story. There wasn't much for me to do besides working on the computer and even that was getting a little tiresome. After spending most of my day on the computer, I wasn't too motivated to spend extra time on it at night, so I stayed in my room and listened to music or went to visit my friends. I also checked out the sunrooms to see who was there I could talk to. I especially liked it when Annie was working because I could sit and talk with her.

One night, I was with her and I happened to mention that I would like to try to get someone to take me swimming again. She told me that she had some spare time and, if I liked, she would be glad to take me. I was thrilled by her offer and accepted it. I was looking forward to spending time with her outside of her job. It made me feel special to be able to share some private moments with her.

We went swimming on the following day. Annie stopped by to get me after supper. I was sitting in the kitchen talking with Henri when she arrived. She asked me if I was ready to go. Henri was a little puzzled because he didn't really know what was going on. He asked where we were going and Annie told him that we were going to swim; so he asked Annie jokingly if he could go and she said, "No way. You are too much for me to handle."

We went across the street to the swimming pool. Once we got there, we were confronted with a problem we didn't anticipate. The pool area had no family change room. I was obligated to go into the ladies' change room. I didn't feel comfortable at all but I didn't have much of a choice because Annie couldn't go into the men's room.

I was nervous entering the premises because I didn't feel like I belonged. Luckily, there wasn't anyone there when we went in. Annie took me into a corner of the room where there was a set of lockers. She started undressing me and suddenly the door opened and a group of women entered the room. They were talking away and then they saw us. The room became silent and I felt completely out of place. At that moment, I wished I was somewhere else. I was really embarrassed! Annie noticed my discomfort and their surprise, so she quickly explained the situation. They were very understanding. One of them even offered to help. While Annie was changing me, we found out that all the women were pregnant and taking a class of hydrotherapy.

After the initial shock of seeing me, the women went on as if I wasn't there. I could hear two of them in the shower beside us comparing the size and shape of their tummies and how they were having trouble positioning themselves to sleep at night. Annie had me changed and ready to go in the pool in no time. As we left the change room, a few of the women wished us a good time in the water; even though, everybody was nice and understanding, I was glad to get out of there.

The rehab center was equipped with a hot tub and a regular size pool. They were positioned next to each other. All we had to do was drive up to an area in between the hot tub and the swimming pool where there was a hydraulic lift; somebody helped to transfer people from their chair onto a chair mounted on the lift. Once in position, it lowered us on either side depending on where we wanted to go. Annie was already in the pool waiting for me as I was lowered in the water. I loved the sensation of floating. It was easier for me to move my body. Annie reminded me of a little girl in the water. She let go of her floating device and paddled her arms and feet like a little dog to keep afloat. She was so cute. It didn't take long for me to get cold and I started to shake.

Annie noticed and suggested that we go into the hot tub. It was great. I felt like I was in my bathtub; it was a warm, relaxing sensation. Our first experience of swimming together was good. We continued to go regularly. I enjoyed spending that quality time with Annie; it gave us the opportunity to know each other better.

Chapter 22

Christmas was approaching and everybody went home for the holiday season. Everyone but Robert, because he had no place to go; I called my parents to ask if it was okay if I brought a friend to spend Christmas and New Year's with us. They were hesitant at first because they didn't know Robert. They were concerned about his degree of disability and what he could do in terms of taking care of himself. They had enough with taking care of me without having to take on an extra load; I reassured them that Robert was fully independent and they agreed to let me invite him. When I asked Robert if he would like to come to my parents' house, he was delighted and excited by the prospect of spending the holidays with us.

My parents came to get us a few days before Christmas. It didn't take long for Robert to settle in. I was always on edge when it came to Robert. He was a little shy and he often compensated for this trait by blurting out the first thought in his head. Nevertheless, Robert fit in well.

I didn't feel well during our visit but I tried to ignore it as much as I could. I had trouble with my bladder. I felt pain in my left kidney; I suspected I had a kidney infection once again.

My godmother came to spend Christmas with us. She was about sixty-five years old at the time. Crazy Robert was making advances on her. He embarrassed me with his often inappropriate comments.

Luckily, my aunt found him to be very flattering. Robert and I listened to and recorded music. I had a big collection and Robert took advantage of the situation to increase his.

My grandmother was cool for her age and she got a kick out of Robert. She thought he was helpful for me, so they got along really well. They and my father were all hard of hearing. It made communication difficult but it was nice to be there with the people I loved.

On Christmas Eve, my brothers and their families came over to open gifts from under the Christmas tree. It was exciting to have everybody there, especially the children. My oldest brother had two little girls and my younger brother had a boy. Everybody had a gift, even Robert. The New Year was a different story because I still had kidney pain. My mother made all kinds of good food but I couldn't enjoy it because I had no appetite. My energy level was way down, so I didn't feel much like celebrating.

My parents drove us back to Montréal after New Year's Day. I felt sick. The trip back to rehab was long and exhausting. I couldn't wait to get back and go to bed.

The following day, I had a high fever and the same symptoms as a few months before. The doctor came to see me, and sent me back to the hospital. I was put on an intravenous solution and given an antibiotic to cure my infection. Fortunately, I only stayed in the hospital for four days. Before leaving, the doctor said it was wise to keep the catheter in until my next rendezvous with the urologist.

I was glad to leave because the hospital care hadn't improved since my previous visit. They didn't wash me, they shoved food into my mouth, and they didn't provide me with any assistance to go to the toilet. It was far from the care I received at the rehabilitation center.

Chapter 23

I was relieved to be back at rehab and my daily activities. I had mixed emotions about relying on a catheter to empty my bladder but, in one way, I enjoyed the freedom of not always worrying about going to the washroom. It took a big load off my shoulders. Some days it was just fine — I barely had to go — but on other days, it was awful because I constantly felt the urge to go. I hated to rely on others to take me to the washroom because not everyone understood my problem. They often made negative comments. It was also a major problem if I went anywhere. I had to be sure there was an accessible washroom and I was with someone I felt comfortable with. Having a catheter was a definite advantage because I no longer had to worry about all those inconveniences. On the other hand, having a catheter made me feel like less of a man. It was a blow to my male ego. I didn't like to have something that prevented me from having a normal sexual relationship.

Three weeks later, I met with my urologist accompanied by Annie. He told me that because of my condition, I had a lazy bladder and I could never fully empty it. And that was the reason why I kept getting infections. He said if the issue wasn't corrected, it could lead to major kidney problems; I asked what my options were. He told me I could either keep the catheter or have an operation that rendered me completely incontinent. I wasn't really prepared to make the decision I was faced with. I didn't like the idea of being permanently incontinent. Such an option for me at the time was out of the question. I couldn't picture myself soaking in urine for the rest of my life. I came to the conclusion that my best choice was to keep the catheter. The doctor told me he respected my decision, but I was at risk of having repeated infections; it was a chance I was willing to take.

Annie sat through the entire conversation without saying a word. We didn't talk about what was discussed during my meeting with the doctor. I didn't feel like talking about it because I hadn't yet come to terms with my decision.

Chapter 24

One afternoon, while sitting in the living room quietly listening to the radio, Martha, our director, and Nellie came to see me to ask if I was interested in going on a trip to Europe. The rehab center organized an exchange with a center in France and they would choose three residents. It would give us the opportunity to learn about their culture and rehabilitation. They thought I was a good candidate and I should sign up. All that was required from the participants was to pay half the cost of their airfare. I signed up and hoped I would be one of the lucky ones to be chosen. I don't know why — you can call it intuition — but I wasn't surprised when I was given the good news. I was excited and looking forward to visiting a foreign country and immersing myself in the culture.

A few days after, Nellie came to ask if I wanted to meet the person who was accompanying me on my voyage. She took me across the street to the library and introduced me to Susan, the rehab librarian. She was a young woman my age and my first impression was not favorable. She didn't speak to me; she spoke to Nellie. Clearly, she wasn't comfortable around me and I don't think she knew what she was getting herself into. Nellie asked her if she knew anything about caregiving and what her responsibilities would be. She said she never provided personal care but she was willing to learn; as for her responsibilities, they were explained to her by one of the trip organizers.

I wasn't impressed by her attitude. I felt she was in it for a free trip; nonetheless, we arranged for her to come over to rehab so Nellie could train her. I didn't understand why out of all the people in the organization, they chose someone with no experience or training in assisting the disabled. Nellie agreed there was something unusual about it. Despite our doubts, we arranged for Susan to learn what she needed to know for our trip. I didn't like the idea of someone with no experience in care giving accompanying me. She didn't know what was expected of her and I was afraid of her reaction toward performing certain tasks. I knew that since she had no previous experience, she would certainly be awkward having to do things related to my personal care and just the thought made me feel uneasy; but it was something I had to go through if I wanted my trip to be enjoyable. Following her first orientation, Susan gave me my morning care twice a week. She did okay but she wasn't a person I really enjoyed being with. We had nothing in common.

Chapter 25

During the first week of March, I had another setback. I was rushed to the hospital. This time the problem wasn't with my bladder or kidneys but my lungs. I came down with double pneumonia. Before I was rushed to emergency, I made Nellie promise that she wouldn't contact my parents to inform them of my hospitalization. I didn't want them to delay their trip to Venezuela because of me. I also didn't want them to worry about me if they decided to go on their trip anyway. Either way, it would inconvenience them, so I thought it best if they didn't know.

My parents planned to stop by rehab to say goodbye on their way to the airport. To prevent them from coming to see me, I devised a plan with Nellie's co-operation. I informed them I was going away for the weekend with François to a chalet in the Laurentians and I wished them both an enjoyable trip.

I was more ill than I thought. I was given, again, a dose of antibiotics. After a week, my lungs didn't clear up. I was taken to the operating room to undergo a horrible procedure which consisted of inserting a large tube down my throat, going in my lungs to clear them out. It was an awful feeling. I was given a mild anesthetic that helped to prevent me from having anxiety.

After the procedure, the doctor prescribed a treatment to be given four times a day by a respiratory therapist. I was lucky if I got it twice a day. I complained to the nurse manager about it and she told me she would try her best to see that I got my inhalation treatments as prescribed; but it didn't happen. The respiratory therapist didn't follow directions; when I confronted her about it, she got angry and told me that I wasn't the only patient in the hospital. She couldn't be everywhere at once and I had to be more understanding. When Nellie came to see me that afternoon, I made her aware of what was said. She wasn't happy. My condition wasn't improving and I needed regular treatments to help my recovery. I had to undergo the same procedure I went through a few days before because of their lack of treatment. I wasn't looking forward to it.

Afterwards, the doctor came to speak to me and told me, if things didn't improve, he was contemplating giving me a tracheotomy. By that time I was tired and upset about everything, and the last thing I wanted was to have a tracheotomy.

When the doctor left, I called Nellie to tell her about my conversation with him. I told her I wasn't getting my treatments done as prescribed and it was the reason I wasn't getting better. She said that she would look into it right away. Shortly after my call, I got a visit from the respiratory therapist and she told me I was put on a priority list and I would get my treatments as prescribed.

Nellie came for a visit that afternoon and told me the director at the rehab contacted the hospital ombudsman to investigate my case. She said she would see to it that I get the proper treatment I required to improve my health. It didn't take long. After receiving my treatments regularly, my condition drastically improved.

My parents returned from their vacation and stopped by the hospital to visit before going back home. Luckily, I was on the mend. I was able to return to rehab after a few days of proper care.

Chapter 26

We were in mid-March and my trip to Europe was fast approaching. Nellie organized a meeting with the people chosen to go on the trip so we could know each other. I knew one of the candidates; his name was George, a young man approximately my age. He had a type of muscular dystrophy with less mobility than me but no visual impairment.

The other person was a woman in her late thirties. She suffered a stroke and was paralyzed on one side, with a severe speech impediment. As for the attendants, there was a male educator whom I didn't know and a female attendant whom I knew. She was attractive, with a beautiful body and liked to flaunt it. She dressed in a provocative way. There were many rumors going around rehab about her. Finally, there was Susan whom I didn't like.

We sat around the kitchen table to discuss our itinerary. It seemed like Martin, the occupational therapist, had it all planned. I thought it was a little odd that none of it was discussed with us beforehand. Susan had a few concerns about the itinerary but Gloria didn't say a word. The young woman, who was paired with Gloria, remained silent during the entire conversation because of her difficulty speaking and wasn't given any chance to express herself. George was very enthusiastic; he had a lot of concerns, questions, and a few suggestions but it was obvious by observing Martin's response that he wasn't really interested in what George proposed.

Martin appeared to be annoyed at George's questions pertaining to his already well-established itinerary.

I left our assembly feeling somewhat unsure about the whole concept. I didn't like the atmosphere around the table. It bothered me so much, I thought it was important that I talk to Nellie about it. When I approached her with my concerns, she assured me that the people who were chosen to accompany us on the trip were there to do just that and they didn't have authority over us. They were strictly there to facilitate our voyage. They would be our hands and legs, and nothing more. They were there to make our trip as pleasant as possible. I felt reassured after speaking with Nellie. I was enthusiastic. I looked forward to going to a different part of the globe.

It was time for Monique, the young lady from France, to return to her country. Before she left, our group of travelers made plans to visit her at her place of employment. I was sad to see her go but I was reassured knowing I would see her again in approximately three months.

Meanwhile, I resumed my daily activities, although I stopped going swimming because I didn't like the idea of swimming with a catheter and a drainage bag attached to my leg in view for everyone to see. I was too proud and hadn't yet come to terms with the fact that I had to depend on a catheter for the rest of my life. It was one more thing I needed to accept but I hadn't yet.

I hadn't had a chance to see Annie since I returned from the hospital because she was absent from work. I missed having her around to talk to. She finally came back after a few weeks. I was coming back from one of my excursions around the block when I heard her voice; it was like music to my ears. I hurried to see her and when I arrived, she was sitting at the kitchen table talking with Henri, Marc, Pascal and Robert. When she saw me coming, she greeted me with a big smile. Everybody was happy to see her back. We decided that we would celebrate her return by ordering out something for supper. It was a good occasion, since Annie was always willing to help. She usually had a lot of time to kill during the supper hour and didn't mind giving us a hand. It wasn't something the attendants were required to do. It was left to their own discretion. Most of them were more than willing to help; but there was always the odd one who complained.

Marc and Henry suggested that we eat at McDonald's and everybody agreed. The problem was that someone would have to go get it. Marc agreed to go but only if someone else would go with him. I volunteered to go because I trusted him. Before leaving, Annie wrote down the order.

Our excursion went without a problem. It was thanks to Marc I made it back safely. We had a good meal and everyone was stuffed. Luckily, Annie and Robert were there to assist because things could sometimes get a little complicated. McDonald's was a nice treat once in a while but it was hard to handle for the majority. We each had a different level of mobility, strength, and coordination. It made eating certain types of food awkward and messy. One thing in particular I liked about being at rehab was it didn't matter how we managed to get things done. It was okay as long as we tried. Everyone had a different way to get the food in their mouth and it was funny sometimes, but between us, it didn't matter as long as we reached our goal. Who cared? The same went for everything else because we respected one another and admired each other's efforts.

Later that evening, I spent some time alone with Annie. We started talking about a variety of things but nothing really important. Annie asked if I would still be interested in going swimming with her. I told her even though I enjoyed the chance to go out and spend time with her, I wasn't ready to go. She asked why. I told her I didn't like the idea of swimming now that I had a catheter; I was having a hard time adjusting. She told me we could always find a way to swim without revealing my drainage system. I told her maybe later on we could try again but for the moment, I wasn't ready. Suddenly, we were interrupted by the sound of Sandra's voice coming from the hallway. She needed Annie to help her with something. Annie left, telling me we could continue our conversation another time.

Chapter 27

Time was long; summer arrived. Most activities at rehab were slowing down and I was waiting to go on my trip to Europe. My hair was getting a little too long and I thought I should get it cut. I wanted to look good to go on my vacation. One afternoon, while having lunch in the cafeteria with Marc and Henri, I happened to mention that I wanted a haircut. They told me they also needed to go for a trim. Marc suggested that we go to Minic's; it was a famous barber shop in close proximity to where we were. Marc said that it was a place where many sports stars went also. If we were lucky, we may see a few celebrities. We agreed to go the next day, right after lunch.

We left at one p.m. the following day. It was sunny and warm. Once again, I depended on Marc to get me where I needed to go. Henri and Robert were right behind us. Robert with his manual wheelchair had trouble keeping up. To make it easier for him, I got him to firmly grip the handles at the top of my back rest. It wasn't a great position but it was better than pushing himself all the way there.

The barber shop was near a busy intersection. I didn't like to be in that type of environment because of the noise from the traffic. I was lost; I didn't know which way to go. I could no longer depend on my sense of hearing to guide me. There were sounds coming from every direction. It made it impossible to orient myself. Luckily,

I could always depend on Marc. Crossing that busy intersection was a scary feeling but it gave me a sense of euphoria. I liked to be around a certain element of danger and conquer my fears.

Thank God I made it safely across. The worst was over, and there were only two more blocks to go. When we arrived, we waited for Minic to come out of his shop with a small wooden ramp to enable us to go inside.

Minic was a jovial man. He welcomed us in with a big smile. His shop wasn't big. There were six barber chairs and Minic was the only male employee there; the rest were women.

Robert and Henri were the first to get their hair cut. Robert embarrassed me once again because he was trying to make the moves on his pretty hairdresser. Henri, who was sitting beside him, thought it to be funny the way Robert interacted with the young lady. Henri had a very loud laugh that drew attention to them both. I could tell by her reaction that she was used to dealing with all sorts, I'm sure she heard it all working in that environment.

While we waited for our haircut, Marc described how the shop was decorated. The barber chairs were made out of baseball bats and the floor was painted like the ice in a hockey arena. There were pictures on the walls of Minic in the company of various stars and celebrities from every spectrum. There were pictures of him with politicians, wrestlers, hockey, baseball, and golf players: all sorts of famous people.

While we were there, the coach of the Montréal Canadians hockey team walked in for a shave and a haircut. The proud barber invited him in right away to sit in his barber chair. Once seated, the barber started to talk to him about the game they played the night before; it brought on a colorful discussion between the two men.

It was finally my turn. The pretty hairdresser was nice and she smelled really good. I couldn't help but notice, while she was cutting my hair, there was a lot of traffic coming in and out of a little back room. It looked suspicious. It reminded me of scenes from an old gangster movie.

We left the barber shop happy. The sun was shining, the weather was warm, and the people who cut our hair were nice and friendly. We made it back to the rehab center without a problem. We took our time so we could enjoy the beautiful day.

Chapter 28

Time arrived for our voyage. We were on our way to the airport. I was feeling nervous. I had never gone on such a long journey and I didn't know what to expect. It was a seven-hour flight and I was hoping I wasn't too uncomfortable sitting in those tiny airplane seats for such a long period.

When we arrived at the airport, Nellie realized she forgot our passports in her office. Our flight was leaving in ninety minutes and it normally took about half an hour to travel from the rehab to the airport. Things didn't start well. Nellie hurried back as fast as she could to get our passports. Meanwhile, we checked in. We brought a lot of material with us, stuff we needed for our personal care, plus our suitcases, so we took advantage of her absence to get that done.

Nellie made it back just in time for us to board the airplane. There, I was transferred on a tiny, narrow wheelchair. It was a difficult experience. Once inside the airplane, there was very little room to maneuver. The doorways were narrow and there was a fairly high step to cross over in the passenger area. The wheelchair barely made it through the incredibly narrow aisle. My seat was in the wing section close to the aisle. It was hard to transfer from the wheelchair onto my seat but we managed. It was the same scenario for the other two who were wheelchair-bound.

I wasn't in a good position; it was a confined area. I didn't have much leg room, and there wasn't a lot of room to recline. Our flight was overnight and we were scheduled to land in Paris at six a.m. I knew as soon as I was settled in my seat, I was in for a long trip. I was nervous, but thankfully, I had a catheter. It would be impossible for me to go to the washroom because it wasn't accessible.

About half an hour into our flight, we got served with a surprisingly good meal. Shortly after, they played a great movie. The flight attendants were wonderful; they were all concerned with our well-being. They were constantly coming over to see if we were okay and I truly appreciated their courtesy.

I tried to rest but I couldn't. I wasn't positioned well enough but Susan was snoring away beside me. I felt like giving her the elbow to wake her up because she was annoying. There I was, trying hard to get some sleep despite my pain and discomfort. It was a long night.

We landed in Paris without a problem; I was surprised to see we weren't directly connected to the airport terminal. Someone was waiting outside with our wheelchairs ready for us to transfer. After, we were put on a bus that took us to the terminal. Once inside, there was someone from the center, where we were going to reside, to meet us. We loaded up the bus with our luggage and headed for downtown Paris. As we got closer, the traffic was heavy. We stopped downtown and had lunch on an outdoor terrace. It was nice but noisy. Then, we walked and checked out a few stores and boutiques, although the majority of them were not accessible; so, those of us who were wheelchair-bound waited outside while the rest shopped. After a long day, we crossed the city to get to where we needed to go.

The center made reservations for us to stay overnight in a youth hostel. It took us two hours to get there because the traffic was unbelievably slow. The bus had no air-conditioning, and it was a hot and humid day. I was tired and having difficulty breathing because of the weather.

When we arrived at the hostel, we went straight to our room. It was a room with three beds. The washroom wasn't accessible. We could go in but not easily. And we discovered, to our dismay, our attendants weren't staying with us. Their room was on a different floor. We told them that it was irresponsible for them to leave us there alone without assistance. If we were in need of help, there wasn't any way for us to let them know. They tried to reassure us by telling us nothing could go wrong and they would make sure that we were comfortable in bed and our needs were met before they retired to their room. Even so, I let them know that I didn't agree with their plans. Martin said, in a condescending way, that he was getting irritated by our childishness and he was hoping that he didn't have to put up with such behavior during the entire trip. We simply had to accept their decision.

The room was hot and humid; it made it hard to breathe. We were transferred in bed and stripped naked. I thought they were being disrespectful but I didn't say anything. I was too tired and angry. Lucy started to make a fuss. Gloria tried to calm her down by telling her it was okay. Lucy made a gesture that she could see us — and she was embarrassed. Gloria replied that she'd better get used to it because we would be living together for the next two weeks.

After settling us in bed, they left the room telling us that one of them would come to check on us during the night. I felt vulnerable; the bed I was in was very soft. It was just like a big piece of foam. My body sunk right into it and it made it impossible for me to move around. I felt trapped, with nowhere to go! I was in a strange country and I had to depend on a group of irresponsible people. That's when I realized I should have followed my intuition — something had told me from the start that they were only in it for the trip.

Gloria returned about two hours later to check on us. They must have thought about what I said because they decided that one of them would stay with us overnight. I was relieved that they changed their minds because it gave me and my roommates a better sense of security. I could relax and get some well-needed sleep.

We woke up early. The attendants quickly got us dressed and into our wheelchairs. I informed them that I needed to go to the bathroom but it was clear they didn't like the idea. They tried to dissuade me from going by telling me that the washroom wasn't accessible and that it was impossible for me to go. George also expressed the urge to go, so I insisted because I knew that it wouldn't be that difficult, if only they were willing to make a little effort to accommodate us. Finally, they reluctantly agreed to take us. It wasn't so hard; it just required a small exertion on their part.

I was getting annoyed by their attitude because they weren't at all trying to meet our needs. We weren't considered a priority to them, even though the reason why they were with us on our trip was to make it as pleasurable as possible for us. It was obvious to me that their priorities were in the wrong place. They were more concerned about their well-being than ours.

During the time I was in the bathroom, the attendants took their shower to freshen up for the day. I found it ironic that they took the time to consider their needs but they ignored ours. I had cramps and I truly felt I needed to go, but despite my attempts, I just couldn't do anything. When Martin returned to help Susan to get me back into my wheelchair, he said to her, "I told you so. I knew he wouldn't do anything."

George got a little intimidated by Martin's attitude with me and changed his mind about going to the washroom. Martin asked him in a sarcastic way if he still wanted to go to the toilet. George said, he no longer needed to go. Lucy had to go but it wasn't too much of an effort for them to take her because she was able to bear weight. After everyone was ready, we went downstairs to have our breakfast. There was a little cafeteria but there wasn't too much for us to eat. They only had fruits, muffins, and porridge. I had to quickly eat my muffin and drink my juice because we were pressured to hurry up. We were running late. Our bus driver was outside waiting for us.

We left the youth hostel at eight in the morning. There was a lot of traffic on the streets at that time. The weather was still very hot and humid, and at the speed we were going, I could tell that we were in for a long day. Nevertheless, I intended to make the best of it. It took us a good while to get downtown.

Once we arrived, we went to visit a few of the major tourist attractions. Our first stop was the Eiffel Tower. Upon our arrival, we discovered, to our surprise, we weren't permitted to leave the bus, for the simple reason that Martin thought it was too much trouble to get us all out for the little amount of time we had to stay there to visit. I couldn't believe what I was hearing. How could he be so inconsiderate?

Once again, I voiced my opinion. I demanded that they get us off the bus, so we could all visit the Tower, but Martin completely ignored me. Susan and Gloria tried to soothe my anger by telling me that they wouldn't be staying too long, only long enough for them to take a few pictures.

They left us behind in a tremendously hot bus. The air was heavy, the humidity was incredibly high, and there wasn't any wind at all. It was difficult to breathe. I couldn't get over how selfish it was of them to leave us there like that. While we were waiting, I took advantage of the occasion to discuss my dissatisfaction with the attitude of our attendants, and from what I could hear, the feeling was mutual. George and Lucy weren't happy with the way we were mistreated either. I told them if they weren't happy, they needed to let the attendants know because if they didn't speak up, they would continue doing things their own way.

We waited about forty-five minutes for them to return. When Martin came back, he said it was a good thing we didn't go because there were so many people that it was hard to move around, and there was a big line to get to the top of the Tower. There was only a small elevator and it probably would have taken us all day to get there.

After we left, we went to take a ride on the river Seine. It was a short excursion that lasted about sixty minutes. It gave tourists a view of some of the major attractions in the city. Places like The Louvre Museum, the famous prison La Bastille, Versailles, and a few more other interesting sites.

We resumed our stay in Paris by visiting Le Montmartre. It was a memorable experience. While there, we thought to have lunch in a cozy little restaurant but as we were about to go inside, an employee came out to greet us and let us know, in a condescending way, that there wasn't room for us inside, even though it was very plain to see that there were plenty of empty tables available. Martin pointed out to him that it looked like they had a lot of free space and the gentleman told him they had reservations. We would just have to find somewhere else to go.

The bus driver told us that such an attitude wasn't uncommon toward the disabled. The general public was still not quite prepared to accept the disabled in the community at large and they were still treated as outcasts. Unfortunately, we just witnessed the perfect example. It was obvious to everyone that we weren't wanted because it was plain to see they had plenty of room for us inside but they were just not comfortable having us there. Susan commented to me after that it was ironic that the French would allow their pets inside the restaurant but they didn't let us in.

We ended up buying some food from an outside vendor who wasn't too far from the restaurant where we were treated as outcasts. We were in a public square inside a very busy area. There were merchants selling things all around us. They sold souvenirs, arts and crafts, flowers, clothing and local foods, etc. There were musicians playing classical music nearby. It was a pleasant atmosphere. After we ate, we stayed to look around a little longer. Before leaving, I had to find a place to empty my drainage bag. We went searching for a wheelchair accessible washroom because there wasn't a discrete area to go. The closest we could find was a very small cubicle. It was only a hole in the middle of the floor. I didn't know that such primitive installations still existed. I couldn't picture myself having to use something like that. It wasn't hygienic. The smell was awful. We emptied my drainage bag as quickly as possible and got out.

After our excursion on La Montmartre, we were back on the bus on our way to the little chronic care center where we would stay. It took us approximately two hours to get there. When we arrived, we were greeted by a welcoming committee. Everybody was there to meet us and they were happy. They gave each of us flowers and a T-shirt with the logo of their organization. Following our introductions, the director of the center took us on a guided tour of the building. It wasn't big but it was beautiful. The main floor had a large kitchen, a living room, and a dining area. They also had a beautiful flower garden in the backyard with a few round picnic tables, parasols, and chairs. The upstairs had ten individual rooms, each equipped with a large bathroom with a wheel-in shower, a bed, and a counter with a sink, microwave, toaster oven, and refrigerator. They also had their own personal items like a television, stereo, dresser, and various other things.

Once we visited the center, the director brought us over to where we were going to live during our stay. It was a separate building, approximately fifty meters from the center. It was a smaller building, with three floors. We were on the lower level. It was a semi-basement and there were steps to go in; fortunately, there was an elevator to go down. The apartment had three bedrooms, a small kitchen, a living room, and a small and narrow bathroom.

George and I were together in one bedroom, and Lucy was in the hallway on a cot next to us. Susan and Gloria were together in another room, Martin had his own bedroom.

We rested before going to the center for dinner. They were very organized for their meals. The staff brought four large pots and placed them at the center of each table. From there, the attendants served everyone directly from the steaming pot. We were served roast beef and gravy, mashed potatoes with beets and carrots. There was cheese, bread, and many different kinds of condiments. It was a well-garnished table.

Most of the residents were able to eat without assistance. Some of them needed a little bit of help cutting their food. Natalie and Marcus both had a severe form of cerebral palsy, and needed to be fed. We were served wine and I was surprised to see that they gave some to everyone. I was intrigued by the way everybody interacted with each other. They were like a close knit family. The director of the center was like a father figure. He was very affectionate and I could tell that he truly cared about his residents and, from what I could perceive, the feeling was mutual.

Once the dinner was over, we sat in the living room with the director to talk about our itinerary. Mister Depardieu, the director, planned a few places for us to visit. He asked us if we liked what he scheduled for us. It was all right by me, since I didn't know too much about the region. Whatever they decided was okay. George tried, on a few occasions, to voice his opinion but Martin didn't give him the chance to speak. Martin was a bit of a bully. He took over the conversation with Mr. Depardieu and anyone else's input didn't matter to him. He was running the entire show.

Mr. Depardieu noticed his inconsiderate attitude and he interrupted him during their conversation to ask the rest of us if we had any ideas. George jumped at the opportunity to say what he wanted to say on several occasions but his efforts were in vain. Martin shot it down by telling George that there wasn't time enough to do what he was suggesting. I thought to myself, How come there was plenty of time to do whatever he wanted but not enough for us? It was obvious to me that he wasn't about to let anyone interfere with his plans. He really didn't care about anyone else, only himself. He was an extremely selfish man and I was beginning to dislike him more and more.

The first night in our little apartment wasn't so good. The air was warm and stuffy. Our attendants got us settled in bed for the night, and after they were done, they took turns taking their shower. They got dressed and ready to go out. I asked what they planned on doing. Martin said they were going out for a couple of hours to visit the city. So, I asked, "What if we need something?" He replied by telling me to stop acting like a child. Lucy tried to speak out but she was ignored. I felt sorry for her. Because of her stroke, she could hardly speak. And due to my visual impairment, I couldn't see her gestures or facial expressions to understand the message she was trying to convey, although it was easy to tell when she was upset because she grunted out loud and tried to speak. They had very little empathy toward her or the rest of us.

Our attendants returned three hours later, laughing and talking loudly, and making no effort not to disturb us. They had no respect and they just didn't care. We got up early in the morning needing care and got a negative reaction from Martin. He told me that there wasn't time enough. I had to insist! Susan and Gloria agreed to help us. The washroom wasn't accessible and the girls had to carry me. We were pressured by Martin to hurry up. We were never given enough time to do what we needed. It had been that way since the beginning of our trip; no wonder we felt stressed because there was never enough time for us in their busy itinerary. We made it on time for breakfast. Everyone was there at the table, waiting for us to begin. Once we finished eating, we all retired to the garden except Martin and Mr. Depardieu, who stayed behind to discuss the details of our daily outing.

There was a beautiful garden in the back. It was surrounded by flowers, mostly roses. There were plenty of flowers but no trees. It was hot that day. Luckily, there were two picnic tables with parasols, but it wasn't enough because the sun was still partially on us and I found it too hot. The heat was draining my energy. I felt sick. One of the girls from the center noticed my discomfort and moved me to an area where there was a little more shade. She gave me a nice tall glass of cool, freshly squeezed lemonade. She was nice and I could see she was concerned about my well-being.

Shortly after, we went on our first excursion. The center lent us one of their accessible buses to travel around. We headed toward the region where part of the Tour de France was held. After travelling for a while, we arrived at our destination. We began to go up a mountain. The climb started gradually but the farther up we went, the steeper it got. There were many little villages along the way. Martin stopped at a roadside souvenir shop. It wasn't wheelchair accessible, so once again we were left behind in the hot and steaming van while our attendants went inside.

The vehicle had no air-conditioner. I asked Susan, before they left to go into the shop, if they could at least take us out of the van so we didn't have to put up with the scorching heat. The van was like an oven. There wasn't any wind. We felt like we were being cooked.

Susan asked Martin if they could get us out, so we could escape the awful heat inside of the van. Martin refused. He told her they wouldn't be gone long and it wasn't worth the trouble to get us out and right back in — we simply had to wait.

They went, leaving us behind. It took them about a half an hour to return but it seemed like an eternity to the three of us who were waiting in that oven of a bus.

When they returned, Lucy indicated to Gloria that she needed to go to the bathroom. Gloria informed her two partners. They had a brief discussion and came to the conclusion that Lucy would have to wait or she would have to use the bedpan. Lucy told them she couldn't wait. She was left with no other choice but to use the pan. With no other alternative, Lucy asked if we, the boys, could get out of the bus so she could have some privacy. Gloria asked Martin if it was possible to get us out of the bus, but he refused.

He said, once again, it was too much trouble and they didn't have the time. Lucy wasn't happy with his response, got upset, and started crying. Gloria tried to calm her down by telling her that we wouldn't look. She had no alternative. I really felt for her. It wasn't right to put someone in such an embarrassing situation. She was only about two feet away from George and I. I felt sorry for her and I was angry at Martin for being so inconsiderate.

It felt great to be back on the road with the breeze coming from the open windows. It gave us a little bit of relief. As we approached the top of the mountain, the incline gradually got steeper. We came across a group of cyclists who were tackling the mountain. It was incredible. I thought it was amazing how they endured such conditions.

We finally made it to the top. Once there, we went to a look-out area with picnic tables with much needed shade from the surrounding trees. We were finally permitted to get out of the bus.

Before we left the center, they prepared a nice cooler full of food and drinks for us, so we took the opportunity to stay for a while and have lunch.

It was so good to be out of that tin box. Martin and George took a little time after eating to take pictures of the scenery. Once we finished eating, we continued on our journey. Only this time, we were heading down the mountain and it was quite the ride: a steep descent, full of sharp turns. It was a little scary at times but thank God we made it down safely.

After leaving the mountain, we headed back to the center. We got there just in time for dinner. Once our meal was over, George, Lucy, and I went out to the garden to get a bit of fresh air. It wasn't very refreshing but it was better than what we endured during the afternoon. We took advantage of the occasion to talk about how we were mistreated. I told them we must be assertive if we wanted our trip to be pleasurable. It was clear if we let them have their way, the remainder of our vacation would be miserable. I told them we mustn't be afraid of them and that the true culprit was Martin. The girls were just followers; I could sense they were intimidated by his bullish attitude. Gloria was a bit of an airhead, and she simply did whatever she was told but Susan began questioning Martin's behavior. It was confusing for her because it was the first time she had taken care of a group of disabled persons. It was obvious to me she was starting to doubt his judgment. She saw his attitude was wrong.

The next morning, we went over to the center before breakfast to take a shower. They had large washrooms, and a comfortable shower chair, and one of the girls from the center helped Susan with our showers. It felt great! It was my first real scrub down since the eve of our departure. After I got freshened up and dressed, we headed down for breakfast and everyone was there, as usual, waiting for us.

I enjoyed having breakfast with the residents. They were a charming group of individuals. They were curious and asked many questions about Canada. It was hilarious because they had a twisted image of our country. They thought Canada was a vast wilderness: that we all lived in log cabins, we still had to hunt and fish to survive, we all wore fur coats and moccasins, and our only means of transportation was on a horse or snowshoes.

After breakfast, we were back on the road again and this time we were heading toward Luxembourg. It was only about an hour's drive from the center. When we arrived, Martin was going around the city trying to find the famous garden of Luxembourg. I didn't know what they were looking for because it was the first time I'd heard of such a place. Finally, after looking around for a good half hour, Martin stopped to ask directions from someone who was on the sidewalk. The gentleman replied, "Well, my dear sir. They are in Paris".

It was ironic to me that Martin made us travel all that distance to see something that was in a different city. I got a little satisfaction knowing Martin got caught with pie on his face; Mister Know-It-All; didn't really know everything after all.

Once we visited the city, we stopped at a small restaurant for lunch. It had a little outside terrace that was wheelchair accessible. During our meal, George mentioned to Martin that when we returned to the center, he would need a suppository because he hadn't a bowel movement in six days, and he was starting to feel sick. Martin told him to let nature take its course; George had to insist.

He pleaded for help, but Martin ignored his requests and that's when I exploded. "We are tired of your attitude and from now on, you will do what we ask. Since the beginning of our trip, you've had it your way and things need to change. Since we left Montréal, there's been no time for us. We are constantly being rushed; no wonder he is constipated because on your schedule, there's no time to even go to the toilet!" I said.

Martin said to mind my own business; it didn't concern me. I told him on the contrary, it certainly did.

"I was informed before leaving on our vacation what your responsibilities are. As our escorts and attendants, you are to do for us what we can't do for ourselves." He answered that I was rude and I should apologize to him. I told him I would not — that he should apologize to us. He went on by telling me if I didn't apologize, he wouldn't speak to me until I did so. I told him I didn't want his help.

Martin helped the girls tie down the chairs securely in the van. When it came to my turn, Martin told the girls they would have to manage on their own because he didn't want to have anything to do with me.

When we returned to the center, it was the same story. Martin helped the girls with my two friends and totally ignored me. I didn't mind. It was okay by me. It was a relief not having to depend on him.

We had supper with our friends at the center and the food was delicious as usual. I was starting to get attached to my French cousins. They were interested in everything we had to say about each other and about Canada.

After we were done eating, George, Lucy, and I went to sit in the living room with a few of the residents. Natalie, the young woman who was afflicted with a severe case of cerebral palsy, indicated to one of the staff she wanted to show us something. The attendant knew immediately what she wanted, so she left and returned shortly after with a small electronic device. She turned it on and placed it onto Natalie's laptop table. The device was equipped with a keyboard and when Natalie pressed a key it gave out an audio response. It took her a while, but she managed to type out a sentence and it read it out loud.

I was impressed by the technology. It helped people who had difficulty communicating orally. It eliminated a lot of frustration. My first thought was Michael and how convenient it would be if he had such an instrument to enable him to communicate. It would open doors for him and it would help me to know him better. I thought it could be a good tool for Lucy also.

When we returned to our residence for the night, Martin put George in bed and gave him a suppository. The girls had a bit of difficulty putting me to bed, but they managed. Ever since Martin refused to have anything to do with me, it made it more difficult for the girls, but it suited me just fine. I despised him. I was happy I didn't have to rely on him for anything.

We got up early the next morning to take our shower before breakfast. The girls got me up and ready. They helped each other with taking care of Lucy and I. Martin only took care of George. I pitied George, having to rely on Martin for all his needs, but he was a little more attentive toward him since our altercation.

It was the fourteenth of July, Bastille Day, a big day for the French. They celebrated throughout the country. It commemorated the storming of the Bastille on July fourteenth, 1789. The storming of the fortress was seen as a symbol of the uprising of the modern nation and of the reconciliation of all the French inside the constitutional monarchy.

We were invited to celebrate at a nearby city an hour north from where we were. Mr. Depardieu organized the day. We were to go to the city hall to meet the mayor and other dignitaries. When we arrived in the city, the festivities were already underway. The houses, businesses, and buildings were all decorated with bright colors. There were people everywhere. We spent the afternoon downtown. There was a beautiful park with a group of musicians playing. It was pleasant to listen to them. We took advantage of our free time to have a little bite to eat. I decided to try out their fries because I had never eaten real French fries before. I was curious to see if they tasted different from ours. Well, I wasn't very impressed. They didn't taste nearly as good as the ones I was accustomed to. I was disappointed. I preferred our good old Canadian version.

We left the park a little after five because we were supposed to be at the city hall at six o'clock. Someone would be there to greet us when we arrived. The traffic was heavy and we could barely move.

When we approached the area of the city hall, the streets were completely blocked. When we got closer to the barricade, a gendarme approached Martin and asked him to turn around because the area was off limits to vehicles. Martin gave him a brief explanation of who we were and the officer radioed his command center to confirm that Martin was telling the truth. He told us to wait a few minutes and he would let us by.

Once we crossed the roadblock, the city hall was only two blocks away. When we arrived, there was someone to greet us and give us a hand. Inside, we were welcomed by the mayor and his entourage. As usual, Martin took over. He didn't give us the chance to say more than "Nice to meet you" to the people who took the time to introduce themselves. We were invited into a large dining room; by the way Susan and the others were describing it, it was a beautiful place. We were presented with a five-course meal. We were then invited to watch the festivities taking place in the front courtyard of the city hall. They led us to an elevator that took us up to the top floor, onto a large balcony that overlooked the courtyard and the festivities down below. I felt special being there. The French were very hospitable toward their Canadian cousins.

We left right after the fireworks. By the time we got back and settled in bed, it was two thirty in the morning. The next day, we took it easy. We stayed at the center and got up later than usual. It was great to relax and not to be rushed because, ever since our departure from Montréal, we were being pushed around and we never had a moment's rest.

The girls helped me out of bed and took me over to the center for a shower. After doing so, they got me dressed and ready for the day. For lunch, we had a picnic in the rose garden. Everyone was there, even Mr. Depardieu. In the afternoon, we went over to a nearby city to visit a plant where they created crystal objects. There was a small museum where they displayed some of their works. There was an area where they demonstrated how the crystal was made and how their creations were done.

Before leaving, we stopped to visit their local gift shop. It was across the street from where we were. It was convenient for us because we didn't have to get in and out of the bus. We were fortunate the gift shop was wheelchair accessible, but once inside, it was crowded. The aisles weren't very wide, so we were extremely careful not to knock anything off the shelves. I took advantage of the occasion to purchase a little crystal clock for my mother to put on the kitchen wall.

We made it back to the center in time for supper. I enjoyed sharing a meal with my French cousins. Despite their disabilities, they were cool. I don't know if they ate like that every day, but the food that was served while we were there was always delicious. After our return, I asked Susan if she could give me a suppository. She told me she never did that but she would ask Gloria to help. I asked Gloria to give me some time because I would like to try to go on my own. She told me she would come back to check on me in fifteen minutes. I was amazed by her response because it was the longest time I was given to go to the toilet since we left Montréal; I was relieved and grateful toward Gloria.

The following day, we went out with the group from the center to visit a summer camp where the residents went for two weeks at a time every summer. The center could only send two of their residents at a time. The group from the center was going to pick up two of their own and drop off two more.

The day was beautiful. The sun was shining. The sky was clear and there was a refreshing breeze coming from the lake. The campsite was fully accessible. It could accommodate sixty disabled persons at a time. The employees at the camp were warm and welcoming. They knew we were coming and they organized for us to go out on the lake for a ride in one of their sail boats. I wasn't very enthusiastic about it. I didn't really want to go but I felt like I had to. I didn't have a choice because the people who were there were so happy, I had to bite the bullet and go. Two strong men picked me up out of my wheelchair and carried me onto a bench on the boat. I was sitting in between George and another fellow. They put a life jacket on everyone before leaving. I didn't like it from the start; to make matters worse, when we departed from the dock and set sail, the fellow beside me began kicking me. He had cerebral palsy and his condition caused him to have involuntary muscle spasms, so the more he got excited, the more he kicked me.

The wind on the lake was fairly strong and there were many waves that made the boat rocky. I was losing my balance and shifting in every direction. It wasn't a pleasant experience. We spent close to an hour on the lake and when we returned to the dock, I was bruised and exhausted. I promised myself there and then I would never set foot on a sail boat again.

After our sailing, we went to have lunch. The lunch area was like a cafeteria setting. Clients would go through the line with a helper, choose their food, and sit at a table. If they required any type of assistance for eating or cutting their food, there was someone available to lend them a hand.

After we were done eating, we went around the campsite to see the different activities offered. There was a variety for all levels of disabilities; sports, swimming, arts and crafts, and even fishing. I was impressed.

We made it back to the center in time for a cold supper. They had a large variety of cold meats, salads, breads, and cheeses, with ice cream and strawberry shortcake for dessert. One thing I learned about the French is that they enjoyed good food and wine.

The next day, we visited a center near the border into Germany. It was a super large, long-term care institution. The director was there to welcome us. He took us on a guided tour. I found it a little creepy. It was an old building, and the smell was one of mold and mildew. The lighting was somber and the floors creaked; the rooms were small and crowded. Some of the rooms had up to eight beds. We were introduced to a few of the residents. Despite their poor living conditions, most of them seemed to be relatively content but there was one exception. He was a young man who had hydrocephalus.

He wasn't happy to see us. He was sitting in his room when we stopped by. He came out and asked what we were looking at; had we never seen a freak before? He was bitter. When I first caught a glimpse of him, I was scared. He had a huge head, and a small face and body. He looked like a character out of an alien movie. We said hi, but he ignored us, turned, and retreated into his room. I felt sorry for him. He was so angry and jaded. I didn't know his life story but it mustn't have been ideal. He probably spent his entire life inside of an institution. Life didn't seem fair to me at times. Why was it that certain individuals had to suffer and others had it so easy? After I saw him, I counted my blessings. I wasn't so bad after all.

After visiting the institution, we were invited to have supper with everyone in their cafeteria. It was a big place. There were a lot of people there. We had trouble finding a spot where we could sit together. There were people there with all sorts of disabilities. Some were physical, some mental, and others had both. The staff interacted well with the residents. It was probably a good place to be if you had special needs, but I would have liked it better if the building wasn't so old and decrepit; it wasn't a place I would like to call home.

As we left, I felt a little guilty that I could leave and they had to stay behind because again I really couldn't understand why it was that certain people had to suffer and others had it so easy.

The next day at the center, we took things easy. We decided to rest since we were leaving the center the following day to visit Monique at the center where she was employed. We took advantage of the time to pack and socialize with our French cousins. They were very receptive and I would miss them. They prepared for us an appetizing, going away dinner. Mr. Depardieu was there. He talked about how much he and everyone there enjoyed our company, and how we enriched their lives. I will never forget their great hospitality.

We took the opportunity to thank everyone for their kindness and generosity. In a way, I was sad to go, but in another way, I was glad to leave because it meant that I would soon be back to Montréal, away from the stressful conditions caused by our inconsiderate caregivers.

We left early the next morning. We were on our way to see Monique. She was working in the suburb of Paris. It was our last day in Europe. We were leaving to go back home to Canada on the following day. It took a while for us to get there. Martin got lost a few times. We had to stop on a few occasions to ask for directions. After much time and frustration, we finally made it to our destination.

Monique was happy to see us and I was also very glad to see her. She ran over and gave me a big hug and kiss. The smell of her perfume brought back old memories. She invited us in, and introduced us to some of her co-workers and a few of the children that she was looking after.

It was a lovely place. It looked homey. It provided day care to children with special needs under sixteen years old. Monique gave us a tour of the building. It wasn't very big. It had a small gymnasium with a physiotherapy department and an equally small occupational therapy department. After our little tour, Monique took us over to a building next to where we were. It was a small rehab center. She introduced us to the night coordinator who was on duty. After the introductions, she, along with Monique, brought us over to our rooms. When we got there, I was surprised and disappointed to find out that we had separate rooms in different areas. I didn't like the sleeping arrangements at all. My room was isolated from everyone. I didn't have any means to get help if I needed to, but I said to myself, what the heck? I've survived so far. I can surely make it through the last night.

Once we had all the sleeping arrangements organized, we went out for supper with Monique at a local restaurant. I enjoyed her company but I felt a little sad because I knew I would probably never see her again.

We got up early the next morning because Martin wanted to take in a few more of the sights before flying back to Montréal. We were pushed as usual to hurry because they didn't have time to wait. I was fed up with their attitude. I couldn't take it anymore, but I knew I would be home soon and I would no longer be at their mercy; however, before we left, I needed to go to the toilet but I knew it was going to be a problem if I asked to go. It was the same for the three of us during our entire vacation. We were in a very stressful situation. Whenever one of us asked for something, we got a negative reaction.

Nevertheless, I asked, but as expected, the response wasn't good. I told them I needed to go and they would have to take me. The girls helped me over to the washroom. After I was there for a few minutes, Martin said to me that I better do something.

I said, "And if I don't, what are you going to do about it?" He slammed the door and walked away. My time in the washroom wasn't in vain. My stress was gone and it felt real good. I was looking forward with anticipation to returning to Montréal. I missed my friends and family, and I was totally played out. I hadn't had a good night's sleep since our trip started. I couldn't wait to get back to rehab where I was safe and secure, and where I didn't get a hassle every time I asked for help.

Before leaving, we went to the same restaurant from the night before. After our quick breakfast, we went on our way. We arrived in Paris an hour and a half after. We stopped downtown to do a little last minute shopping before leaving to board our flight back home. We stopped at a small perfumery and I took the opportunity to buy something for my dad. After, we had lunch outside at a small restaurant. It had an outdoor patio.

After lunch, we headed straight for the airport. Our flight back was at seven p.m. but we left early to avoid the rush hour traffic.

We arrived at the airport a little after four. By the time we got our entire luggage checked in and had gone through security, we had one hour to wait. We had time to relax and have a snack while we waited to board the plane. It was one of the most peaceful moments we had during our entire trip. We didn't have to hurry; we could relax and just wait to be called to embark.

Our flight back to Montréal went fairly well, even though, I couldn't sleep for most of the way and I couldn't wait to get out of the plane. I was uncomfortable in my seat. I tried to relieve the pain by tilting back my seat to shift my weight around a little to remove some of the pressure. It helped a little; I was so tired that I slept on and off anyway.

Finally, I heard the voice of the pilot, saying we were landing in Montréal in ten minutes. I couldn't wait to get back on Canadian soil.

When we landed, Nellie and François were inside the terminal to greet us. I was happy to see them and I felt a big weight off my shoulders. I didn't want to have anything more to do with our three unreliable attendants. I had it in my mind since we left on our vacation that I would write a report to Nellie about their conduct. I wasn't about to let them get away with the way they treated us. I wanted everyone to know how inconsiderate they were toward us and how much we were neglected.

I no longer had that aspect of vulnerability and I wanted them to pay for their behavior. They had spoiled it for us. We could have had a terrific vacation filled with fond memories but instead all I could recall was their selfishness.

The person I despised the most was Martin and I didn't want to let him get away with his pompous demeanor. I wanted him to realize his errors and to suffer the consequences. He didn't have authority over me anymore. I wanted everyone to know what he did, and for him to feel some sort of shame and remorse regarding his unacceptable behavior.

Chapter 29

When I arrived back at rehab, I went straight to bed, I was exhausted. I slept all night and woke up the next day at eleven a.m. Nellie decided to let me sleep in. She knew how tired I was. When I was up and ready, I headed down to the cafeteria to get a bite to eat. I got my food and went to sit with my buddies. They were all there as usual, sitting at the same table. I was glad to see them, and judging by their remarks, they were also happy to have me back.

After lunch, I headed straight down to the computer lab to work on my report of the events that took place during our voyage. I wanted to write everything down right away while it was still clear in my mind. I spent the next three days writing about it. I didn't want to miss a thing. I wanted to make sure everything I wrote was accurate.

Once I checked and double-checked my report, it was time to present it to Nellie. After reading it, she handed it over to the coordinator. The following day, I was called into the coordinator's office. When I got there, my report was on her desk in front of her. She told me what I wrote was troublesome, and if it was true, she would certainly see to it that the people involved were reprimanded. She said that she would have to verify with Lucy and George to see if my accusations were well-founded and she would get back to me when she had all the facts straight.

A week later, the coordinator called me back in her office to let me know that she spoke to everyone involved and she believed me. She told me that Lucy and George confirmed all that was divulged in my report. She said she was sorry and it was unfortunate that our trip wasn't more pleasant. She ended our meeting by reassuring me that the persons involved would be held accountable. I found out later on that Martin got a three-day suspension but the two girls didn't get anything. I was disappointed because I didn't feel vindicated.

With my trip behind me, I resumed my work with the computer. Things were quiet because many people were on vacation. There wasn't too much to do. The computer was no longer a challenge. My time at rehab was coming to an end. The only thing that kept me there was that I was waiting for the arrival of my new wheelchair. My occupational therapist thought it wise that I remain at the center until I got my chair and the proper adjustments were done before I left. I was just killing time until then.

One day, Pascal came to ask if I wanted to go for a ride with him. I told him I would, but only if he didn't go too fast and he let me know when we arrived at a crossing. He promised he would look out for me. I wasn't persuaded but I decided to go. It was a sunny day and it would give me the chance to be outdoors. He took me to a little park. The trip there wasn't bad, although Pascal kept on going too fast for me. I had to keep telling him to slow down. He would speed up to an intersection and wait for me to get to him before he continued on his way. I figured at the time, he didn't realize I needed to remain close behind him in order to know where to go. Anyway, despite my difficulty, I managed to make it to the park safely.

The park was quiet. There weren't too many people there. We stayed for a while. I found Pascal was acting strange. After a while, Pascal said to me, "Do you remember when I told you someday I would get you back for all the times that you teased me? Well, this is my payback."

He took off, leaving me behind. I felt scared; I was left there all alone in an unfamiliar place and I wasn't sure I could make it back to rehab on my own. I waited a while, hoping Pascal would return, but he didn't. I had no other choice but to try to get back on my own. I headed back slowly, trying to recall each step we took along the way. I wasn't very brave; I took my time and kept my cool. And I managed to make it back to rehab safely.

My biggest fear was when I got to a crossing. I never knew if the sidewalk had a ramp for the wheelchairs or not; I took a chance every time, hoping it was okay. Thank God, things went well.

After that incident, my relationship with Pascal wasn't the same. I didn't trust him. I don't know what was going on with him, but he was bitter. He didn't find pleasure in anything.

He was about to leave rehab to go to live alone in his own apartment, with twenty-four hour care on site; even though he kept telling everyone that he couldn't wait to go, I could tell he was scared and putting up a front.

Pascal left about two weeks later, but as I suspected, things weren't going smoothly for my little buddy. He didn't adapt well to his new environment. He felt alone, scared, and insecure. He couldn't sleep; he was extremely anxious and sick. His parents took him back home. He wasn't feeling well at all; he got double pneumonia.

Nellie took Robert and me over to visit him at his home, and he wasn't good. He was on some kind of respirator. His breathing was shallow and he wasn't very alert. Due to his condition, we thought it best not to stay too long. We said our goodbyes and wished him well, although I somehow knew it would probably be the last time that I saw my buddy. I felt scared, sad, and helpless seeing him that way.

Pascal passed away a week later at the age of twenty-one. I miss my friend. He was truly an original. There will never be another one like him. I won't forget him.

Soon after Pascal passed away, Marc moved out of rehab into an apartment similar to the one Pascal was in. I felt sorry to see him go, but I was happy for him. He finally got what he wanted.

I was the next to leave. I was going back home to live with my parents. I didn't like the idea but I didn't see any other alternative at the time. I was scared and didn't think I could make it on my own.

My new chair arrived and all the adjustments were done. There was nothing more for me to do there. I returned home after spending twenty-eight months in Montréal at the rehabilitation center. My time there taught me a lot. I learned to be more assertive and not to be taken advantage of in different ways. It helped increase my self-esteem and made me unafraid of asking for what I needed. Before I was admitted at rehab, I hated to ask for certain things in fear of being too demanding or a burden. I had a way of making my condition more difficult than it was. I was too proud for my own good. My time at rehab made me a little wiser. It also made me accept my situation and try to make the best with what God gave me.

Chapter 30

My going back home was quite a change. I organized most of the care I needed with the local community services. They provided me with the funding to hire my own caregivers, which meant I had a choice. A number of people came and went. Eventually, I got two workers, a man and a woman. They became my regular caregivers. They were reliable and did a good job. They enjoyed what they did.

My physical condition was worse than before I went to Montréal. I couldn't eat on my own; I needed more help with everything. I couldn't get dressed by myself, and I needed bowel and bladder care. I had an indwelling catheter that needed to be irrigated every day. My caregivers came in the morning to get me up and ready for the day, and returned in the evening to put me in bed. I could no longer make it up the stairs to have supper with the family. They brought down my meals and fed me.

I didn't like it; I caused a lot of worries and anguish. It was a stressful period for everybody. I was alone most of the day with nothing much to do. I wrote on my computer or listened to the radio and TV, and that was all. I was isolated. I went from having a fairly busy life in Montréal and being surrounded by people, to living alone at home with nothing to do and no one to see.

I was depressed; I kept to myself and I hardly talked. Why should I? I didn't have anything to say. I was trapped in a body that didn't work and confined to a wheelchair with no hopes or ambitions, with nothing to look forward to but my condition getting worse. I knew how much of an impact my condition was having on the rest of the family. They didn't know how to deal with me or the situation; it was a rough period for all.

Finally, the moment I was waiting for and I feared the most arrived. I received a visit from a social worker telling me that my parents could no longer deal with me, I had to move out. I was shocked, angered, and disappointed. Even though I knew the time would soon come. I wasn't prepared to leave home and family, and be isolated and secluded from everyone. I would no longer be a part of the homestead. I felt worthless and rejected. I was a burden they wanted to get rid of.

Out of sight, out of mind. It was easy. Get rid of the problem and everything would be fine for them, but I couldn't escape from myself and my difficulties. I had to deal with them every day no matter what. I had to face them because I didn't have a choice. From that moment on, I knew I was alone. If I wanted to survive I needed to be strong. I couldn't just simply give up. From that day on, I learned not to depend on anyone. That way I wouldn't be disappointed.

Chapter 31

Six months after the dreadful announcement, I was admitted into a long-term care institution in Ontario: away from home, out of province, away from friends, away from the rehab center, away from everything familiar. It was the hardest day of my life. My room was small with two beds, which meant I was sharing my room with someone. It had a very small closet and a little dresser for both of us to share. There was no bathroom; we had a small sink in the far corner of the room beside a little window that faced the front street. That's what my entire living area was reduced to. The building was old and it smelled. It was an awful situation to be in. I needed to remain strong and not let it get to me.

My first impression of the people who worked there was one of control because from the first day, they gave me a list of rules and regulations. I had a long battle to face because the attitude was one of authority; they weren't used to being told what to do. They were more in the habit of imposing their will on the people that they were supposed to accommodate. I needed to change their attitude if I wanted to survive in that jungle.

They wanted to decide when I got out of bed, when I went to the bathroom, and when I went to bed for the night. I had to make them understand that they were not dealing with a confused, old person. I was a young man with all his mental capacities, who was able to voice his needs.

They were a little too set in their ways, and it was due time that they changed their perspective because they had it all wrong. It seemed that we, the patients, were there to accommodate their needs instead of the opposite. It was a view I was determined to change. They had it too easy. They constantly rushed to go on their break and made the patients wait until they returned. They often left them in bed all day; even though the patients wanted to get up. It was a sad situation at times. There was also a big lack of dignity and respect toward some of the patients. The more vulnerable suffered the most. I promised myself that I would do my best to change the situation and to restore dignity, compassion, and respect.

It angered me, the way those poor, old gentle souls were often treated. It was unacceptable that they didn't get the respect they so much deserved. They were people who worked hard all their lives to make our country what it is today. The freedom that all of us can enjoy is thanks to those elderly people. They fought in the wars for us to have all the rights we take for granted.

It didn't take me long to know the ways and the people. Shortly after my arrival, they were holding elections for the president of the residents' council. I previously attended a few of the meetings and I found that there wasn't much happening with important issues, so I decided that I would run for election to try to change the attitude and ways of the workers in the establishment. I ran a campaign like they had never seen before. I was running against an elderly man who had been living at the institution for many years. He acted like he was my arch enemy. He didn't like me at all. One day, I met him going into the elevator and he told me that I wouldn't win the elections; that I was just a young punk and I didn't stand a chance because he had been living there much longer than I. He told me, everybody knew him and no one in their right mind would vote for me; therefore, I'd better quit because it would save me a lot of embarrassment.

That meeting prompted me to campaign even more; I wanted to win. It was an opportunity for me to make a positive difference and I wasn't about to give that chance away. I was determined to show him I wasn't a pushover. I made posters and put them up all over the hospital. I wrote, printed, and personally distributed pamphlets at every patient's room, and at the same time, I took the opportunity to meet with them, and to talk to them about their care and about what they wanted to change. It wasn't easy because the majority of the people who were living there were not cognitive. We didn't have a large number able to vote, even though the institution at that time had five hundred and thirty-five residents. If I won the position, I intended to take my role as president of the residents' council seriously because the well-being of the residents would partly be my responsibility and I didn't intend to let them down.

Finally, after a month of hard campaigning, the ballots were counted, and the results were very close. I won with a majority of twenty-one votes, and my opponent wasn't very happy. He stormed out of the hall, telling me I was just a punk and I didn't know anything.

After a few days, I went over to see my rival and told him that he was right, that I didn't know too much about the politics within the hospital, so it would be a great benefit to me if he would be willing to work with me to show me the ropes, and that his wisdom and knowledge would be welcomed. If we could work together, we could do a much better job.

Chapter 32

So began my struggle to make things better. It wasn't easy because I often had to calculate my words whenever I spoke to some of the nurses or to the administrators who would come to our residents' council meetings to hear our concerns or opinions on certain matters. They were a very touchy group and they didn't like any type of criticism.

From what I could tell, before my arrival, the residents' council was just a formality. They didn't have much power at all.

I was determined to change that way of thinking because I wanted them to listen to our concerns and to do something about them. From then on, they were going to take our needs seriously and do something to improve our situation. I wasn't going to let go until they were no longer an issue. They had to change their attitude because we weren't there to facilitate their lives; they were there to take care of us and our needs, and to make our lives easier.

While I was there, I was approached by one of the occupational therapists. She wanted to start a newsletter for the patients to keep them entertained and aware of what went on throughout the hospital. I thought it was a wonderful idea. It would give me a perfect venue to write my opinion on certain matters that concerned me.

We had a small group of patients who took part in the newsletter group. We met every Friday afternoon. We didn't have too much material because the residents couldn't really write their own articles; therefore, we would often find articles from other authors and put them into our newsletter. The first article that I wrote brought on much controversy. Some liked it and agreed with what I had to say, while others were totally offended.

Here's what I wrote:

BAD ATTITUDE

Some people come to work every day with a bad attitude. People have to realize that living in an institution is not an easy thing. If you do not like your job, why don't you quit because you are only making our lives miserable? Thank God for those who care, but unfortunately, they are forced to take on most of the workload because of those who come in with their bad attitude.

In turn, it is the loving, caring, and supportive staff that end up injured and burned out. Unfortunately, because of unions, the system protects them. We are constantly having to battle with certain people to get what we need.

Staff needs to realize they are here for us, to meet our basic needs, and to make our lives easier. If we were not here, they would not have a job. We are being called clients and, in any other profession, the client is always right. If they were employed elsewhere and treated the clients the way they treat us, they would not be working very long, but it seems that in this environment, they can get away with a lot and without any repercussions.

I realize that some of you who read this article may be offended. I understand that working in healthcare can be difficult but this is our home and we are here twenty-four hours a day, every day. We don't get to go home after an eight-hour shift to relax, unwind, and escape the noise, stress, and the whole environment.

Our second edition of the patients' newsletter prompted me to write another controversial article.

During that summer, the employees went out to the garden to take their break. I would sit and listen to people around me complaining about their work. It made me frustrated because no matter what part of the garden I went into, there was someone complaining about their job.

MY JOB

Hi, readers! I would like to tell you a little bit about my job.

I started my training at the tender age of twelve; although I was not quite ready to undertake such a gruesome career, I had no choice in the matter. As the years went by, I became an expert in my profession. I must admit that it is not an easy job at times. I am required to be on duty twenty-four hours a day, seven days a week, with no vacations. The pay is below the poverty level and there are no fringe benefits.

It's a job that requires me to work constantly with the public, which means I have no privacy whatsoever. I am forced at times to deal with unsympathetic people, and to always be patient and smiling, no matter what.

I perform most of my duties sitting down. It gives me a chance to listen and to talk to different people. I find that most people are not happy with their jobs or with their lives.

Even though my job is not an easy one, I have learned a lot about it throughout the years. It has made me more patient and understanding. It has also given me a good sense of values.

I started working at this job over twenty years ago and I have now just about reached the top of my profession. I suppose you are all curious to know what my job is all about. I am a Certified Visually Impaired Quadriplegic, and let me tell you, it isn't an easy job. It can be very difficult at times, but I've learned to enjoy life no matter what, so for those of you who are fed up with your job, why don't you quit? I wish I could have the same option.

The patient newsletter was discontinued shortly after. The occupational therapist who was responsible for overseeing it quit, and no one replaced her. I personally believe that she was advised to stop because not everyone agreed with what I was writing. My tool to voice my opinion was taken away.

It was that way for everything. Almost every time I tried to make people understand our concerns, they undermined my efforts. Especially with matters involving nursing. Their attitude was, "How dare you criticize our nursing practices? We are highly professional and we are looking out for the well-being of our patients." I was often angered and frustrated with their hypocritical attitude. I witnessed, on a daily basis, nurses leaving patients in bed — justifying it by saying that it was best for the patients; saying they were tired and could use the rest; some days they got them up and left them in their uncomfortable wheelchair all day, sleeping or crying. It was peculiar they weren't so concerned with their well-being then.

They often said to some of the most frail and vulnerable patients who wanted to get out of bed, "If I get you out of bed now, you will have to stay up all day, until after supper." Given that option, most would remain bedridden because it was simply too hard for them to stay up for such a long period of time. In reality, they didn't have any choice. Thank God for the nurses with empathy. Thanks to them, I survived in that crazy jungle.

The people from recreation, occupational therapy, and pastoral care helped a lot. I often talked to my pastoral worker about my frustrations, and fears. I looked forward to meeting with her every week. I opened up my thoughts to her. We had a special rapport. She made me understand that God was always with me. He was there to help me. Having faith helps. As president of the council, I called on His guidance and asked Him to send good people my way.

The department of most resistance was nursing. They were reluctant to accept constructive criticism.

Our first battle was sanitation. We had several discussions with the nursing administration and the cleaning department so the caregivers were no longer allowed to enter the rooms with dirty diaper bins or leave them sitting in the hallway. Privacy and dignity are always a problem in shared spaces. Our main complaint was the night shift; they talked and laughed loudly, left the lights on, moved noisy carts and went on like it was the middle of the day. They listened to the evening report at a volume that everyone could hear. There was no consideration whatsoever; they did what they needed to do and that was it.

We complained to deaf ears about the constant and casual breach of confidentiality.

There was no toilet in our rooms. We used a commode chair separated by a thin curtain. People came in and out without any respect for privacy. It was embarrassing at times. People walked in on me when I was being washed. They just didn't care.

Our biggest and ongoing complaint at the residents' council was the constant lack of response to call bells. They always said our complaints were unfounded and exaggerated. I think it's a problem that may never be fixed. They had better things to do with their time, like sitting at the desk and talking on the phone with their friends and family, going on break, or laughing and talking with their colleagues. It made the patients more insecure. It prompted them to yell and cry, and to ring the call bell more frequently. And for those who couldn't ring the bell, it made them call out in a loud voice or cry for attention. I didn't get much rest there.

There was a young woman who moved into the room facing mine. She was the mother of three little children who suffered a stroke while giving birth to her last child. She was totally paralyzed on one side and she lost her speech.

One night I heard someone entering the young woman's room and turning on the light; the young woman was grunting and complaining. I overheard the sound of a man telling her he was going to change her diaper. She started to cry.

She cried during the whole embarrassing ordeal. It angered me. It could have easily been prevented because there were female nurses on duty. Why did they have a male nurse take care of such a young and vulnerable woman? They had no empathy. They didn't care; the patients were treated like objects without feelings.

Chapter 33

I met and befriended many patients during my stay. They were all special to me in their own way. They all had their own ways to contend with their situation. Some were bitter and angry, while others accepted their fate and tried to be happy. Life inside long-term care isn't easy. People cope the best they can, even though the majority were admitted against their will, with their rights taken away. They had no alternative because their families could no longer handle the increasing amount of care. They had no other choice but to place them into an institution, and hope they got good care; but in most cases, it was inadequate. Others had nobody and were left alone to die. It's sad that some people spent the remainder of their lives that way.

There was a patient in particular who was extremely bitter and angry. She was a woman who immigrated to Canada from Europe a long time ago but still kept her Czechoslovakian accent. She rarely spoke, and when she did, it was to insult someone. I often met her going in and out of the elevator. The first time I had the privilege of meeting her, I was going in the elevator and as soon as she saw me, she said, "You are not a man. You do not wear shoes."

She startled me. My first reaction was to say, "Hi, sweetheart, how are you today"?

She replied, "I'm not your sweetheart. I'm nobody's sweetheart. You're crazy." It took a long time for me to gain her friendship, although whenever people witnessed us together, they would think that she despised me, but I knew that deep down in her heart, she had a warm spot for me.

There was also a younger woman in her mid-forties who suffered from multiple sclerosis. I often met her in the hallway during my physiotherapy or at the occupational therapy department. She was timid. When the weather was nice, she was stuck inside. When I saw a volunteer, I got them to take her out to enjoy the weather.

One day, while talking to her in the garden, I asked why she didn't have a power chair. She said she would love to have a motorized chair because it would give her a lot more freedom. The next day I was at a meeting with my O.T. and my little lady's occupational therapist happened to be there. I couldn't help but confront her. She replied by telling me it wasn't my business. I told her she gave me permission to talk to her, so she explained to me that she wouldn't benefit from having a motorized chair. I asked why. She said it was better for her if she continued to push herself around to keep her strength a little longer. I told her, "Who are you to decide what's best for her?"

A few months after, my little lady received her motorized wheelchair. After that, we could see her everywhere. Seeing her with her new powered chair really made me happy because her situation no longer seemed as bleak. She was a lot more outgoing and had more energy to get through the day.

There were all kinds of people who had different types of medical conditions. Some were worse than others; although, I believe that the ones who suffered the most were the ones who had their entire mind and were fully aware of what was going on with them. It was a scary thought that somebody's mind may be fully present, but they had no means to communicate their thoughts and wishes: to have strangers think and decide for you without any way to express your discontent or disapproval.

Chapter 34

One day, I was outside in the garden enjoying the fresh air, the sun, the peace, and quiet. I often went there to escape the usual noise, the smells, and the hustle and bustle of the hospital. One of the recreational therapists came over to introduce me to a young woman in her early thirties. I tried my best to make her feel welcome. I didn't have anyone who was young at the hospital with whom I could relate because everyone there was either too old or senile… I saw the opportunity to make a friend.

I continued doing my work as president of the residents' council. I enjoyed it and it kept me busy. There were many changes going on, and my job was to see that throughout those changes, the residents wouldn't be directly affected.

It was a rough time for healthcare. I was asked to participate on an advisory committee held by the provincial government to minimize the impact caused by the drastic cutbacks. I was glad to have the opportunity to voice my opinion. I attended half a dozen meetings on the matter, although I quickly realized their choices were already made. The government in power obligated the institutions to reduce their costs of operation.

To make matters worse, the hospital began some major structural changes, starting with the kitchen. They also needed to destroy our little garden where the patients went to occasionally have barbecues, or just went outside to enjoy the warm summer weather and escape the craziness inside.

It was quite an adjustment. The quality of the food diminished. The system wasn't ideal. During that period, the institution received a large amount of money from the government to do some major renovations. The hospital was old and in need of change. I attended many meetings on the subject. Despite the fact that changes were needed, we were in for some major disruptions. It wasn't going to be easy and the patients were the ones who would suffer the most, as if they didn't have enough problems.

I needed to escape from the whole environment. I missed the water. I thought it would be good for me physically and mentally. I met with the head of the volunteer department and voiced my desire to go swimming. She said she would contact me as soon as they found someone to help me.

Meanwhile, I asked the recreational department if they could get someone to accompany me. Luckily, one of the girls in that department was willing to do so. Everything went well and she seemed very comfortable with what she needed to do. I felt confident and at ease with her taking me.

Our first outing went well. With the buoyancy of the water, I was able to move my limbs a little and it felt great to have no pressure on my body. What a relief! I could feel the blood circulating everywhere. The water was warm and cozy. I loved to be in the pool! Another thing I liked was that I got to take a shower. Because at the hospital, we were only allowed one a week. The rest of the time we were subject to a bed bath, and it was basically a lick and a promise. I also enjoyed having lunch after at the canteen in the lobby of the pool. It was a pleasure to eat something different than the same old hospital food.

I continued swimming once a week. I looked forward to my outing. It was my chance to get away and be part of the outside world.

My recreational therapist continued to accompany me swimming until the volunteer department finally found someone. She was a big girl, tall, and husky. The first time we went swimming, my recreational therapist came with us to show her what to do. Our first time alone went fairly well but I didn't feel at ease with her. I wasn't comfortable having such a young person seeing me in the nude; however, it didn't appear to bother her.

One afternoon, a friend came to visit. We were having a beer and talking. Suddenly, a nurse walked in and politely informed me in front of my friend that it was prohibited to have alcoholic beverages inside the patients' rooms. I was embarrassed. After my friend left, I asked the nurse to come over. I needed to speak with her. I said to her, "How dare you come into my room and embarrass me in front of my friend? This is my home and if I want to have a drink in my home, it's my choice. And it's none of your business."

She said I wasn't following the rules, so she was obliged to intervene. I told her that she was forgetting one thing — that the hospital was my home and that in my home I should be allowed to do whatever pleased me. She told me that she was strictly obeying the rules and she didn't want to get into trouble.

I met with the medical chief of staff a few days later. I was surprised by her interest in what I had to say. I basically told her that everyone keeps emphasizing that the hospital is the home of the patients, so we should be allowed to do as we choose in our home without having imposed on us a multitude of restrictions. My two main concerns at the time were the drinking issue and the visiting hours. If this was really our home, it was high time that they made us feel like we were in a home and not a prison.

Two weeks after our meeting, I received a letter from the chief of staff informing the residents' council that alcohol would no longer be prohibited in the hospital, although it mustn't interfere with doctor's orders, and that visiting hours would also be lifted as long as we didn't disturb others. I was happy with the outcome of our meeting. We were finally making some improvements. I was beginning to feel less powerless and like I could make a change. It encouraged me to do more to better the lives of the residents.

I decided to visit the young woman I met a few days earlier in the garden. She always kept her door shut. It made it difficult to approach her but I finally got the courage to knock at her door. I asked if she would like to come out into the garden with me. I persuaded her to go; but she needed time to get out of bed and in her chair.

We sat under a big tree, enjoying the weather, and getting to know each other. I found her sweet. I liked her right from the start. Even though there were things about her that were unusual to me, I could live with them. I was lonely and I welcomed her friendship. It didn't matter if she was different. I needed a friend: someone I could confide in.

We hung out together most of the time. She wasn't always easy to get along with because she could be moody. I was starting to feel more for her than friendship. She was pure and innocent. I decided to take my time before I tried to push our relationship further.

The hospital was about to undergo a major overhaul, which meant that I was fairly busy as president of the residents' council, I attended several meetings related to the renovations. It was a major undertaking and the people who would suffer the most would be the patients.

The first stage really hurt! Despite an overwhelming amount of protests, our wonderful chapel was destroyed, even though for many it was considered the heart of the hospital and a place of refuge. I, and many others, liked to go there to escape the noise and hectic life. It was one of the many changes that we as patients had to accept and deal with. It had a devastating effect on all of us. Every time they started and completed one section of demolition and reconstruction, they dispersed patients to different areas of the hospital. For many it was traumatizing to leave an area which they were used to. I had to listen and address several concerns from the residents during that period.

There was an old lady named Shirley whom I befriended. She was very warm and sweet. She had an advanced form of Parkinson's. She was fragile and her unit was going to be the next area renovated; she was very worried about having to be transferred. She died two weeks after the move.

Shirley was a Jewish woman, very maternal, and always concerned I wasn't eating well enough. She occasionally showed up at my door with some fruit or other types of food to make sure that I was eating well. I took it upon myself to order out restaurant meals at least two or three times a week. It didn't take long for the word to get around; many residents came to have me order them food. I knew every restaurant telephone number by heart, every delivery person by name, and every menu and price of each item. I came to know everyone's preferences.

The hospital had a good recreational department with devoted individuals. Their purpose was to entertain the residents. It was a good opportunity for the residents to get away from the nursing care and be treated as humans, not as patients or numbers. They had things to do like arts and crafts, board and card games, bingo, Valentine's Day, Mother's Day, and other monthly celebrations throughout the year. Trivia was very popular; we would even have competitions with other institutions. Accessible buses took us to outside activities such as restaurants, outdoor festivals, shopping and concerts. It was a pleasant change from the normal routine and helped to alleviate pain, worry, and stress.

We were privileged to have an elevator operator in charge of the main central elevator. It was, for many of us residents, practical and necessary because most of us couldn't access or operate the elevator on our own. We were informed that the position of the elevator operators would be eliminated. We at residents' council were disturbed by their lack of consideration. I started a petition to keep our elevator operator. I got an overwhelming amount of signatures and our plea wasn't ignored. They recanted on their decision and everybody was happy with the outcome. I was probably the most happy because all of my efforts weren't in vain; at least I could do something positive.

I was approached by the head of the psychiatric department to take part in a project he was about to undertake on abuse and neglect in long-term care. It was a national project in collaboration with five different provinces. I was glad he considered me and I accepted. It was a subject I took to heart. I witnessed many types of abuse and neglect conducted in a very subtle way. Some caregivers weren't even aware at times of their actions but others were perfectly aware.

The project lasted a year. It consisted of literature and a couple of videos on the matter. Judging by what our establishment learned by viewing the material, it seemed to have a positive effect; but despite the efforts made, it was totally useless for some. They were very good at doing a bad job and covering it up.

I contacted the local CNIB to help me with my computer. All I could do with it at the time was read and write. I was hoping their volunteer department could find someone to teach me how to go on the World Wide Web. They found a young man in his early twenties. He was a real computer geek. It didn't take him long to have my computer set up so I could go on the Internet. The computer systems at that time weren't geared to the disabled. The voice output system only worked for text. With the Internet, there was much more than just text, so my usage was limited to e-mail; however, it permitted me to communicate with people everywhere.

My young computer genius took me out of the hospital to go shopping, to movies, and to restaurants. We even went to a rock concert. He came around to see me regularly for approximately a year, until he took a job outside of the city.

My new volunteer was Amanda; she was shy with a good sense of humor. We began to do many different outings together and I really cherished my time with her.

I hesitated to ask if she would like to take me swimming. If I sensed that she wasn't at ease with the situation, it would also make me uneasy; but luckily, she was okay with it. The first time we went was a little awkward but soon we were okay with each other.

One day, she invited me over to her home for a barbeque. The house where she lived wasn't wheelchair accessible, so it was held in the backyard. Upon our arrival, Amanda introduced me to her friends. They were both from Argentina. I felt special to be among such beautiful women. The first thing I knew, it was time to return to the hospital. I dreaded the thought of having to go back to the suffering and craziness, but I didn't have a choice. It was my home.

At least, I tried to make it my home but I couldn't. Every time I went somewhere out of the institution, it was more difficult to go back. I hated the environment and I didn't feel like I belonged. I was isolated from my family and people I loved.

One day, the elevator operator advised me that my old friend Frank was expected to pass away at any moment. When I entered his room, I didn't know what to say. I simply prayed to God that He did what was best.

Frank died later that evening: a man who was alone in life. He had no kin, and the only people who took the time to know and care for him were from the institution. With health reform, many of those caregivers lost their job; therefore, a lot of frail people gave up. It was too much for them to start over with a new group of people. It was sad because the government implemented those measures without knowing the impact.

One day I heard about a project Frank was trying to realize. It was constantly delayed by bureaucracy, policies, and regulations. I thought it was a good idea, so I decided to take it on. I met with the head of the recreational department. I asked what exactly was needed in order for the project to become a reality.

Despite her obvious reluctance, she told me if I got her the tools needed, she would see I got what I asked for.

I was determined to see my old buddy's idea become a reality. Soon after, residents were able to enjoy our happy hour five days a week. I enjoyed going there to visit and unwind, and have a few beers with the people there, such as patients, volunteers, and the recreational therapist.

I really liked my girlfriend and I wanted to push our relationship further. She told me she never had a boyfriend or even kissed a boy, so I decided to take my time before I revealed my true feelings. One particular evening we were talking, when suddenly, I interrupted her and asked if I could kiss her. She said yes but she didn't know how. I told her I would be happy to teach her. From that moment on, our relationship grew stronger. I accepted her constant mood changes and her bizarre ways because I loved her, and I needed the love and affection she gave me.

At the same time I was admitted to the institution, François began volunteering. He was a truly amazing man. During my stay he helped me to eat my dinner daily; he barely missed a day. He sometimes assisted up to seven patients during suppertime.

He also went on outings with clients to medical appointments, shopping, and to different recreational activities. He occasionally brought us some of his home-made donuts, cookies, macaroni, and chicken soup as a treat because he knew how monotonous the hospital food was. François gave his love and devotion to those in need, and that is what made him so special.

François was one of a kind. He suffered from a severe heart condition, but despite his frail health, he chose to give a good part of his life attempting to relieve the loneliness and suffering by showing his unconditional love to the residents.

Chapter 35

The living conditions inside the institution were making me extremely tired. I could hardly sleep at night. I had no privacy whatsoever. The food wasn't good. The conditions took their toll on me and I came down with pneumonia. My oxygen level was low and my CO_2 was very high. I was on the brink of death. The local priest came to give me absolution.

My mother arrived shortly after and she was clearly upset. She questioned the nurse as to what they were doing to improve my condition. The nurse told her the doctor didn't prescribe any medication. My mother insisted they call an ambulance. I was disappointed my father wasn't there. I tried to console myself; he probably didn't come because he couldn't bear to see me suffer.

Upon my arrival at the hospital emergency, I was quickly examined. I was put on antibiotics for ten days. It didn't take long before I was feeling much better. Despite my improved condition, the doctor thought that it would be best if I remained in the hospital for the full course of treatment until my infection was completely cleared up.

I returned to the institution feeling better. My energy level was way up. I was ready to tackle any obstacle. I had another project I planned to undertake — our small coffee shop that catered to residents and employees. People often went there to have a drink and snack: the usual stuff like coffee, candy bars, and soda. It was a place to relax and escape the craziness of the institution.

With the new food production, we, as residents, wanted more food options because the meals weren't very appetizing. The portions were often too small, the quality declined, the food was too cold, too dry, or it was unappealing, but there was no choice but to eat it. My project was to get a better variety of food in the coffee shop. With the approval of the council, I began to seek out ways to make my idea a reality. It was decided management would stock the coffee shop with a variety of already prepared foods; it wasn't what we had in mind but it was definitely an improvement.

I had a good friend and roommate Wally for three years; I felt like his son. He was an old man in his late seventies who suffered from a stroke and dementia. He lived in his own imaginary world and, let me tell you, he had a vivid imagination.

Every day was an adventure for Wally. In a certain way, God had mercy on him; even though his body was confined to a hospital bed, his mind wasn't there.

Things were not always rosy for Wally. He sometimes had a lot of pain, and whenever he did, he cried like a baby or howled like a wolf. It was impossible to keep him quiet. Eventually, they medicated him to calm him down.

Wally had a good sense of humor. One day he had a bad cough. I said, "Wally. You'd better do something about that cough." He answered, "It's not the cough that will carry me off; it's the coffin." The only person who came to see him was his daughter. It's sad how someone's life could change so drastically.

Despite his condition, Wally had a good appetite. The center put him on a soft food diet because they were afraid he would choke on a regular meal. Wally loved hot dogs and almost every day he asked me to get him one. He was so happy when I brought him one that it didn't take him long to gobble it all up; after that, I frequently brought him a hot dog and he was always grateful to get it. It was a special treat for him. I was glad to see I could do something to make him happy.

Sometimes, I went out and came in late, and Wally was awake waiting for me. When I arrived, he gave me the third degree. He said, "Now. Where were you? Do you know I was up worrying myself sick about you?" It felt good to know someone cared about me. Wally took sick one day and they sent him to the hospital. It was the last time I saw my old friend. Although he passed away, he still remains in my heart.

My next roommate was a man in his late sixties who suffered a massive stroke and didn't appear to have any brain function. I wondered why some people had to suffer like that. I prayed God would take him away so that he no longer had to live such a miserable life. There was pain and suffering all around me. I coped the best way I could. I tried to keep busy. I needed something to distract my mind or else I would go crazy. I thanked God every day for giving me such a strong mind and the resilience to go on.

I liked having my girlfriend present in my life. She gave me warmth and attention at a time I needed it. Yet she really frustrated me at times. As our relationship progressed, she made a lot less effort to go out; she would cancel our plans at the last minute. She would rather fight with the nursing staff instead of going out and having fun to forget all the worries of the hospital. We were slowly drifting apart. I was getting annoyed by her behavior but I didn't want to lose our relationship. I loved her and I enjoyed the trust and intimacy we shared.

Chapter 36

Life inside the institution was getting to me — driving me crazy, in fact. The noise, lack of privacy, the smell of dirty diapers, the cold from open windows, a lack of empathy from the staff. It was hard to sleep and to find comfort. What kept me going was my work as president of the residents' council, and going out to different activities and outings in the community. I was lucky to have a good group of friends, which helped me to cope.

During the evening, I often went downstairs to the little boutique to get myself a snack, and to get away from the stench and noise of my unit. That's where I first met Chantal. She was working at the boutique. I was very impressed with the way she interacted with the people she served. She had a way to make the people around her feel good. I was delighted by her attitude because most people weren't as comfortable as she was around severely disabled individuals. We ended up becoming very close friends. She was a joy to be with. It was thanks to her and many others that I could survive the institution.

I often went down to the basement to a favorite little spot I found inside the furnace room where it was warm and I wouldn't be bothered by anyone. It was often very cold inside the hospital during the winter season.

There wasn't a single place in the entire institution where a resident could have any privacy. I found it extremely annoying. There wasn't any place where my girlfriend and I could have a quiet moment together, without being disturbed. My next project was to approach the hospital planning committee about the possibility of a room that would be reserved for the use of the residents and their friends and family. It would be a place where people other than staff could go to have a private conversation: a place where couples could go to share some intimate moments together without the fear of getting caught in an embarrassing situation.

They were surprisingly open to my request. It wasn't realized right away but, in the meantime, I managed to negotiate a temporary haven for us: the most important item of all was a door with a lock to assure the privacy of the occupants.

Because of a new government regulation, the residents who smoked cigarettes or any other type of tobacco products would no longer be allowed to do so. As you can imagine, this didn't go down well with the residents who smoked. The residents' council once again stepped up and worked with both sides. They were all up in arms with the coming rule, stating that the institution was their home and they should be exempt from the new regulation.

I received valid arguments from both sides. There were the non-smokers who wanted the new smoking regulation reinforced and the smokers who definitely wanted to keep the status quo. Finally, after a few months of discussions, we came to a reasonable compromise. The institution agreed to allocate a special room inside the hospital for smoking. It didn't make any sense to me that some human beings would choose to destroy what little health they had. For the majority, it was a very positive change.

Amanda, my friend and volunteer from the CNIB, informed me one day after swimming that she simply didn't have the time to volunteer any longer. It was always disappointing when a volunteer moved on. I wasn't quite persuaded I would see her again but despite my doubts, she did come by when she could. I loved having her as my friend. My self-esteem was low during that period and for me to have such an intelligent young woman as a friend helped to really increase my morale. I don't know if Amanda realized how much I appreciated her friendship and how much she helped me through a rough period.

One afternoon, I received a surprising visit from Amanda's roommate. Vicky, one of the girls I met at the picnic, from Argentina. I was surprised, thrilled, and happy she came. She was in Canada to learn English. Like her friend and roommate, she was very intelligent. She didn't remain in Canada long after I befriended her. We continued to communicate by way of the Internet.

One day, while visiting Chantal at the boutique, she told me she was going to Montréal to study at Concordia University. I hated goodbyes, especially when it was someone I truly loved and cared about, but I went on her last day anyway. I was greeted by the same cheerful welcome I was accustomed to. She was busy training a personable young woman to take over, but I wasn't very interested in knowing her because she would just leave like everyone else. I was bitter and I decided from then on not to get emotionally attached for fear of getting hurt again.

One warm summer afternoon, I was in the rear of the hospital cruising around in my power chair, trying to keep cool. While turning the corner, I hit the curb. Upon impact, my chair went up on the curb and it caused me to lose my balance. I couldn't breathe and I was afraid my chair would fall right over. I thought for sure I was about to meet my maker. Suddenly, out of the blue, my friend and buddy Danny showed up.

Danny was a middle-aged man who was afflicted with cerebral palsy. His condition had rendered him deaf and mute. I was trying to tell him to go to get help. To my great surprise, he managed, with difficulty, to get off his scooter, stood up beside my chair, lifted it right off the curb, and straightened me back in my wheelchair! What a relief. I was delighted and amazed by his heroic gesture. I never thought he was capable of such a feat.

I was frustrated with the attitude of the residents. They didn't do anything to improve their care and living conditions. Very few came to our monthly residents' council meetings. It made it difficult for our suggestions to be taken seriously. Residents were often afraid to speak up in fear of some sort of retaliation, although they often came to me to solve their problem. The more the patients who could speak up did so, it wouldn't only help improve their living conditions, but it would also help the poor souls who couldn't speak for themselves.

I was at a crossroads in my life. I felt very unsettled. I was reliving a lot of past hurts that I thought I had dealt with: feeling let down and discarded like an old shoe, the lack of privacy, the controlling environment, the lack of empathy, being placed in an institution, feeling isolated and worthless, not feeling loved or cared for, feeling like a burden, feeling like an outsider, wanting out with nowhere better to go.

I never really got over being disappointed in my family and friends. I realized it wasn't easy for them to see my health deteriorating to the point where I lost my independence. I understood the decision to put me into a long-term care institution wasn't easy for my parents, especially my mother. She could no longer cope with the stress of having me at home. They honestly believed the institution would be good for me.

But from that moment on, I knew I had to take care of myself. I was blessed with a strong mind. I decided to take every loss or obstacle that came my way as a challenge. It was a way for me to cope with all the changes happening to me.

On top of everything else, my girlfriend was driving me nuts. I could no longer see the point of being involved with her. We were too different in many ways. I had to let her go or else get caught up in her negativity. It broke my heart to break off our relationship but I knew it would be completely unhealthy for me to stay in her environment. It seemed to hurt me a lot more than it did her. We still cared for each other and we remained good friends.

My younger brother came to visit me one day, which was an unexpected surprise. Beside my parents, he was the only other person in my entire family who occasionally came. We sat in my room in front of my computer playing Yummy. He had just completed detox. As part of his rehabilitation, he needed to apologize. As far as I was concerned, those were normal things that happened between brothers. I accepted his apology and I told him I loved him. He said we would see each other again soon but he committed suicide a few weeks later. It was a complete shock! My first reaction was deep sorrow; later it was anger. It was such a dark time for me, trying to cope with all of my losses and difficulties, but still I managed to enjoy life enough to keep on fighting despite my fears and anxieties. I found it incomprehensible that he gave up. It took me a while to come to terms with his death. It was unfortunate that he didn't find an alternative to end his suffering. I loved my little brother, Bruce, and his death left me with emptiness and sorrow.

My next project as president of the residents' council was to motivate the resident community. My idea was an award. It took a little work, but eventually, the award was created. It consisted of a plaque that stated: "In recognition of their dedication and hard work toward enhancing the quality of life of their fellow residents and friends."

The first recipient was a man in his late fifties afflicted with cerebral palsy. He was dependent on others for everything but always willing to help.

Instead of feeling sorry for himself, he did what he could to improve his quality of life. It is hoped that by becoming the first recipient of the Paul Seguin award, he would inspire others to do more to improve their lives and encourage others to follow.

Loneliness resurfaced on a regular basis. Who would want someone like me — someone severely disabled? I would probably remain single for the rest of my life. It was a hard pill to swallow. Every night, I prayed to God to send me an angel; a beautiful woman who would love me for myself.

People from my past seemed to have deserted me. So, I was truly surprised and delighted when I received an unexpected visit from a person that I had known for many years. Neil wasn't like me. He had a troubled life, but despite his tough exterior, he had a soft heart. I could see it by the way he befriended me. With me, he wasn't afraid to reveal his vulnerable side.

Neil was always getting himself into trouble with drugs and anything imaginable where he could make a fast buck. We reminisced about times gone by and we talked about people we knew. I never saw my buddy Neil again.

I received a call from my mother about three months later telling me that Neil committed suicide. I felt sad; once again I had to figure out how to deal with loss. I never could comprehend why perfectly healthy people couldn't contend with the difficulties of life. I truly believe that we were all put on this earth for a reason and that we had to face whatever obstacles came our way, even though, it often seemed like there was no way out.

We all have a choice about how to live our lives and, regardless of our condition, we can choose to have a positive attitude or spend our lives miserable, feeling sorry for ourselves. I decided at an early age I wouldn't let myself get to the point of giving up: that I would face any challenge that would come my way. I learned to appreciate everything our dear Lord gave me. Having said that, being in the institution was trying. I continued as president of the residents' council but administration was resistant to change, especially nursing. They were set in their ways and we were considered troublemakers. Change was slow to come, but it did eventually materialize and those changes had consequences. I felt a lot of animosity from some of the staff; they made my life much more difficult than it needed to be.

Chapter 37

I was so unhappy. I was so lonely but when I befriended anyone, it didn't last. I tried not to get attached but I ended up letting my defenses down and letting them into my heart, leaving myself vulnerable. But what else could I do? I needed the friendships. They kept me sane. I decided despite my fear of getting hurt, I would enjoy my friends while I could instead of worrying about if they would let me down. I had many people come and go. I didn't have anyone I could truly rely on. I didn't have any sense of belonging; I felt like I was drifting. I felt like an outcast with no hope for the future. I didn't see anything positive.

What kept me going was the residents' council with the many meetings that I had to attend because of the renovations. My physical condition was a lot worse. I had almost no movement except just a little in my right arm and my head. The rest of my body from the shoulders down was paralyzed. Besides driving my chair, I was totally dependent on others; the prospect of losing all my independence scared me. It was the only freedom I had left and I wasn't prepared to forfeit it.

One afternoon I went to visit Kim. When I arrived, she was talking to someone. Her name was Maura; she had a very strong accent. She was from Brazil and she was showing Kim a video of her country. She told me if I stayed, she would do her best to explain what was on the screen.

I was pleasantly impressed by the way she explained everything. She was full of passion and pride. I liked her. She was empathetic and compassionate. She liked to help people and it gave her a good opportunity to speak English. Her volunteer job consisted of putting away the patients' clothing brought up by the laundry department, but it didn't give her much opportunity to speak and learn English. I jumped at the opportunity to teach her English. I liked her and I wanted to get to know her better. We made arrangements to meet every afternoon.

After she left, I couldn't wait to see her. She was so sweet that I couldn't resist her charm. I felt like I was setting myself up to get hurt but she was worth the risk. I tried my best to conceal my excitement because I didn't want to scare her away. I sensed she didn't know much about the disabled. I needed to see how comfortable she was around me before I could let her into my heart.

We did a lot together and I relished every moment with her. What impressed me was how comfortable she was despite my disabilities. She didn't mind assisting me with what I needed. She found pleasure in helping me, and I enjoyed her care and affection.

My self-esteem was low and I honestly didn't think anyone would have feelings for me other than friendship. I felt like a burden. I didn't think I was worth having. Why should I? I was put aside by everyone. If my friends and family didn't care to keep ties with me, why would anyone else want me?

Maura began to speak to me in French. Her accent turned me on. She gave me a very passionate kiss. I let go of my defenses and returned her kiss with just as much passion. We thought it was best to find some place more private, out of the detection of staff and clients. We were in love and it was a great feeling.

I was afraid that given my situation, she would eventually get tired of the restrictions caused by me being institutionalized and go away. But things were going just fine and I was deeply in love. Even though I was very physically disabled, she didn't mind helping me. I was more accustomed to having people that made me feel like I was a pain but with Maura I didn't feel that way. We went sometimes to the patient family room for privacy, away from the scrutiny of the staff. My love for Maura was growing stronger and I wanted to be with her all the time. After the day was over, she went home and I stayed behind in an environment where I didn't belong. I didn't find any joy there.

It was unfortunately time for me to train a whole new group of caregivers. My new team was just horrible. I had to struggle to keep what little independence I gained. My team leader was the worst. I had to constantly fight to defend my rights. She was a control freak.

Early one evening, the team leader said if I didn't go to bed right away, I would have to wait for the night shift. I didn't like her attitude; she wasn't going to impose her will on me. I refused to be intimidated by her. I told her she would put me to bed at my regular scheduled time. She left declaring that it was my choice but I would have to wait.

I was upset with her pompous attitude. I ended up going to bed that evening at my regular time without a problem, although the team leader didn't show up to help her partner. It was clear she wasn't happy with the outcome and it wouldn't surprise me if I endured some kind of repercussion because of my defiant attitude.

I planned before knowing Maura to go to a rock concert with my friend Michelle, my favorite recreational therapist. I didn't feel so well that day, I didn't know if I could make it through the day without feeling any worse but I would go to the concert anyway. I tried my best despite my ill feeling to enjoy the concert and my time spent with my sweet friend. I was anxious for the concert to be over. I wasn't well and I just wanted to get to bed.

The following day, I didn't feel better. I was worried. After supper, a nurse came to give me my medication as usual. When she put the pills in my mouth, there was something different — there were more than usual. I spit them out. I asked what she gave me. I discovered that she gave me two extra pills. I told her that nobody advised me about any changes in my medication and I refused to take it. She told me I was within my rights.

The following day, I confronted my new team leader, Marie. I told her, she had no business giving me medication without advising me beforehand; I said I would speak to the head nurse about it if she did something like that again, but deep down, I knew, if I did so it was pointless because the head nurse was always on the defensive whenever anyone said anything negative about her personnel. She was a troublemaker. I didn't like her and it was clear she didn't like me. The atmosphere was cold whenever she was on duty. I really don't know why she was so bent on making my life difficult. My life was so much easier when she wasn't there. A lot of the nurses helped me despite her warnings because they knew she wasn't right.

Maura and I were close. I thought about her all the time. She came to do her volunteer work every day during the week. Once she was done, she came looking for me. She usually found me at happy hour having a beer. Maura was quite the socialite. She loved people and loved to lend a hand whenever she could. She was pleasant to be around. Sometimes we went somewhere quiet, away from onlookers so we could have intimate moments together. However, those areas were hard to come by. It was hard to have a relationship inside the institution. We went everywhere together and did a lot — we were clearly in love. It was kind of strange that she was able to see beyond my disability for who I really was. To her, I wasn't simply a person who was a burden to everyone. She loved me like I am. I could let all of my defenses down with her.

I wanted to get out of the institution. With Maura in my life, I didn't see how our relationship could last with me there. I loved her more than I had ever loved anybody, and the thought of losing her was frightening and painful.

I had previously made steps to get out of the institution and to live in the community in my own apartment with caregivers on site twenty-four hours a day. I had some doubts and reservations because I wasn't sure I wanted to live alone. After living inside an institution for such a long period, I didn't know if I could make it on my own. During the six years I was there, I was used to having everything done for me such as my laundry and cleaning. I also didn't have to worry about my meals, groceries, or bills to pay. It made me insecure just thinking about all those responsibilities and I had a fear of becoming isolated again. Moreover, I didn't receive any encouragement when I expressed my desire to leave. I said to myself I would deal with it when the opportunity arose. Now I had Maura in my life and it was a whole new world. I could envision us living together because I loved her dearly and I didn't want to lose her.

After struggling with my thoughts for a while, I finally asked Maura if she was willing to move in with me despite the obvious problems. Despite all my fears and doubts, she said she loved me and she would gladly move in with me no matter what the problems may be. I began to investigate my options to leave the institution.

The process for me to move into the community wasn't easy. There was a long waiting list for supportive housing. I couldn't wait to regain my freedom. I contacted every agency I knew to speed up the process to be with Maura; we wanted to be with each other.

Maura awoke something in me I worked hard to suppress for several years. I was scared and uncertain, but at the same time excited. I was sexually attracted to her and I wasn't quite sure what I could do about it, given my physical condition. It was difficult; I focused more on my inability to perform adequately instead of enjoying the tender moments we shared. Maura was patient and told me she loved me no matter what, and I should enjoy what we had. But, deep down inside, I was still not comfortable; we consulted a doctor and he fixed the problem.

I loved Maura more than I ever loved anyone and I wanted to share the rest of my life with her.

Maura and I kept our plan to move into a supportive housing unit a secret until we had everything organized so as not to worry our families. It wasn't normal to many people that a beautiful and intelligent young woman like Maura could love someone like me. There were all kinds of gossip and rumors about us, and we were constantly being scrutinized. I couldn't wait to get out of there and into the privacy of our own home.

During most weekdays, Maura was busy with her volunteer work and I was busy with my work as president of the residents' council. I did what I could to keep myself occupied until Maura and I could get together after our daily commitments. Whenever I wasn't busy with meetings, I was running around visiting some residents who were mostly bedridden. I felt sorry for them because the majority didn't have family or friends to visit them. If only more people took time out of their busy schedules to listen to those poor souls, it might change their perspectives. The people I took the time to visit all had very interesting stories to tell. They made me realize that family and friends were the most important things in life.

Chapter 38

The rest of that winter, I kept occupied with the affairs of the residents' council and doing a lot with Maura outside the institution. I didn't feel well but I didn't let it stop me from doing as much as I could. I was afraid if I stopped, I would be at the mercy of the staff that didn't care if I lived or died. I would simply become another statistic.

I was having trouble with my right arm. I was afraid if I lost the only movement I had, I would lose what little autonomy I had left; I would no longer be able to maneuver my power chair. I would become completely immobile. I asked my occupational therapist for help. We came up with something that made it a bit easier but it was just temporary. It made life extremely stressful because I never knew if I removed my hand from my joystick whether I was able to get it back on.

The summer season finally arrived. It was a pleasant change for many to have young volunteers around. They were so full of life and energy; it was a joy to have them mingle with the patients. They had barbecues and ice cream parties. The happy hour was outside when weather permitted. They often took residents on outings, to restaurants, outdoor festivals, concerts, and baseball games. It was a nice time for those who were able to participate, but I pitied the residents who were stuck inside lonely and bored, and at the mercy of the people administering their care. The heat was often unbearable inside because the building had no air-conditioning except for the administrators' offices.

My love for Maura was unbelievable. I never loved anyone as much as her. When we were apart, all I did was think of her. She was my pride and joy, and I wanted to share every moment with her; but with me living inside an institution, it was just not possible.

During my stay at the institution, I befriended the spouse of one of the patients who was living there. Karen often complained about the level of care her husband was receiving. She constantly had to remain vigilant so that Ian got what he needed.

Ian and Karen used to operate a Bed and Breakfast in a cozy and quaint little village approximately forty-five minutes from Ottawa. I introduced Ian and Karen to Maura, and they soon became friends. Karen asked Maura and me to spend the weekend with her in her home. It was fairly accessible and it would give us the opportunity to be together.

The weekend was great. We had our first chance to spend the night together and I was a happy camper. After that weekend, I was determined to accelerate my plan to move out. Every week, I called the local community support service providers to see if they had any vacancies and where I was on their priority list. They told me that since I was housed in an institution, I was high on their list because living inside an institution wasn't considered appropriate housing. I was on the top of their list. I simply had to wait!

The summer went by fast. We were already in the fall and I still hadn't heard from the supportive housing group and I was getting extremely tired of my living conditions. I just wanted to get out of there as soon as possible. Thank God, I had Maura to distract me. I wanted to be with her all the time. I was tired of us having to leave each other at the end of the day. It was frustrating for both of us.

Maura did a lot of things for me that the nurses didn't have time to do; instead of being thankful, they often tried to stop her from helping me. Their attitude made me angry because to them, as patients, we weren't allowed to have the same privileges as them. Nevertheless, I did my best to ignore their comments. They had no compassion whatsoever. Flu season arrived. Many of the patients died and a lot of the frontline staff was home sick. Due to the influenza outbreak, many of the floor units were quarantined. We were understaffed and our movements throughout the institution were restricted. It wasn't a pleasant atmosphere. I was lucky because I was one of the few who didn't get the flu.

Christmas was approaching, and Maura and I planned to spend Christmas Day with my parents. The flu epidemic made things a lot harder for me because there wasn't much to do. Mostly all the activities were on hold, and the time was long and boring. I couldn't wait to see my family and eat my mother's cooking.

When we arrived at my parent's home, my dad came outside to greet us. Their home wasn't wheelchair accessible and when I went to visit, I used my manual wheelchair so my father could lift me up onto the little front veranda to get into the house. Despite my dad's good will, I could see it was strenuous for him; but with Maura there, I felt like less of an imposition. I knew that she loved me despite my condition and the rest didn't matter to her.

We had something between us that nobody could really see or understand. She loved me for who I was and as I was. She saw much more than the obvious obstacles that faced us as a couple.

Our Christmas gathering was great. My mom's cooking was as delicious as usual and everybody enjoyed Maura's company. I could tell my father in particular liked her. It wasn't hard to understand because Maura was beautiful with an amiable personality. I loved her so much and I was proud to have her as my girlfriend. She gave me a sense of worth, which I hadn't felt in a long time.

Maura's family planned to go back to Brazil for six weeks during the festive season. Maura couldn't afford to go; we took advantage of the time to be alone together. It was nice that we didn't need to go our separate ways come nighttime, and I didn't have to deal with the hostile and regimental environment of the institution.

After spending time alone with Maura, I had to get out of the institution and live with her, although I had no choice but to wait and pray that I would get a supportive housing apartment soon. I wasn't happy with the way things were going. I wanted to be with her but I was losing hope.

One day, I received an unexpected call from the executive director of an organization that provided supportive housing in the community, telling me they had a unit available and she wanted to interview me to see if I fit their program. After I hung up, I felt somewhat scared but thrilled at the thought of living with Maura. I was a little insecure because what if she changed her mind? She didn't. We still had a lot to worry about before our wishes were reality.

The following week, Maura and I met with the executive director of the supportive housing committee and her new assistant. The interview went well.

The Monday following our interview, I got the call telling me I was accepted in their program and I had approximately a month to move in, or it would go to the next person on their waiting list. I was excited but it didn't give us much time to prepare for our move. Maura was worried about breaking the news to her family. We decided it was preferable not to say anything before we actually moved. As for my parents, we kept quiet until everything was finalized.

I went to see my occupational therapist, for advice on to facilitate my transition. She was helpful and cooperative. She was keen on doing what was best for me. She never imposed her will. The most important thing on my list was an environmental control unit. With such a device, I would be able to control everything I needed in order to function as independently as possible in my own home. The problem with getting the ECU was the cost.

I got a visit from a columnist from the Ottawa Citizen newspaper. I explained to him that without the ECU, it was unsafe to move into my own apartment. Dave Brown put out his column a few days after his visit. It didn't take long before the money started pouring in from everywhere. It was just incredible how Dave's newspaper column had such an impact on his readers. People sent me cards of best wishes along with their contribution. They were all cheering me on and they were very supportive.

After that week, the donations practically stopped. We were fearful I wouldn't reach my target of twelve-thousand dollars on time. Dave's second article about me was a tremendous help. In addition to the public's contributions, I also received a generous amount of money from the Senator's alumni, Motion Specialties, and the supportive housing organization where I was to move. All in all, I received fourteen-thousand dollars. It was all overwhelming for me. Everything was happening fast and it was almost too good to be real. My prayers were answered.

I learned that a small group of nurses were planning a potluck dinner for Maura and me as a going-away present. On the day of my going away party, the nurses in question had everything arranged. Every single one of them went through the trouble to prepare a nice dish for me. They also decorated their small meeting room and they organized the table for us to share a nice meal. Unfortunately, it wasn't to be. One of the girls came to tell Maura and I that our little going-away party was cancelled. The nursing manager found out about it and said that if they continued their plans, they would be subject to disciplinary action. It was disappointing.

It was very frustrating that despite my efforts in the last seven years, certain people and attitudes didn't change. It was a cruel and unnecessary act. A few of the nurses told me bluntly that I would be back within a month. I wasn't about to prove them right.

The day of my big move finally arrived. The nurse sat me down on the commode chair and left to attend other patients. She forgot to fasten my seat belt and I fell straight on the floor, head first. I fractured my femur once again and I pulled out my indwelling catheter. It made quite a ruckus. I was completely dazed. A couple of nurses came to my rescue. They picked me up from the floor and put me in bed. Despite the pain, nothing was going to stop me from moving that day. They couldn't do more for me than what Maura could. After they put in a new catheter, I stayed in bed a little while to gain my composure. Maura was a little worried upon her arrival but I reassured her I was fine. I was happy to leave that stressful place and I wasn't going to wait a moment longer. Before leaving, we said our goodbyes to everyone who took the time to see us off. I was glad to finally be leaving. My move was something I had planned ever since the first day I arrived.

What haunts me is that there is still a significant number of young, physically-challenged individuals who remain in the same kind of situation I was in. I lived inside the long-term care institution for seven years. When I arrived, I was overcome by the rules and regulations, their regimental attitude, and their complete lack of respect. All around me were people suffering and dying. It wasn't a healthy environment.

I thought I was there to die. I didn't want to be there.

I didn't belong! During my stay, I discovered that I wasn't the only one in that situation. There were many younger patients who, like me, simply did not belong in that type of setting but we weren't given any other option. There was no other place to go.

It has already been close to ten years since I left the long-term care institution. I must admit it was scary when I first moved. When I was living at the institution, most of my needs were provided. When I left, I wasn't quite prepared to face the outside world. It was a whole different environment. I came from a place where I had to fight for everything and where I didn't have much say as to how my care was administered: a place where they preached dignity and respect, but it was rarely practiced . When I moved into my apartment, it was a whole new ball game. I regained control of my life. I am now able to direct my care, eat what I like, make my own decisions, and have a somewhat normal life.

I married Maura two years after we moved in together; I thank God every day for sending me such an angel. My life has taken a complete turnaround since meeting her. Despite my disabilities and my progressive illness, I have never been so happy. I believe we all have a purpose in life and no matter how difficult things may be, we have to be happy and appreciate what God has given us. I am the perfect example of what God can do. Keep the faith because there is no telling what God has in store.

Since I had the opportunity to move out of the institution and into the community, I've been doing a lot of volunteer work. I have a much better social life and that's why there has to be better alternatives for people in long-term care. I wish our government would put money into programs like the one I belong to, so more physically challenged individuals like me could be given the same opportunities. Our government's decision not to put money into similar programs like my supportive housing has forced a lot of people to remain unnecessarily stuck inside a hospital, or some other kind of institution, waiting to die. It has been proven that it's much more affordable to have people living at home than to have them clogging up our hospitals and long-term care facilities. It would give individuals who are disabled a better life. There aren't enough units to support the needs of the physically challenged and the waiting lists are long. I believe everyone in our society should have the right to a better life. If given the chance, many of these people would benefit by living in the community.

These are my thoughts, my perspectives, and my world as it is...

I look to the horizon and I infuse a quote from George Bernard Shaw:

"You see things and you say, 'Why?' But I dream things that never were and I say, 'Why not?'"